T0306154

HOW TO HAVE A SUCCESSFUL FREELANCE EDUCATION CAREER

Teaching and education offer a hugely rewarding career – but staying in the classroom for life is not always right for everyone. With a successful teaching career under her belt, Fe Luton made the move from classroom to kitchen table, entering the world of freelance education writing, research, and training as a general all-round creative.

How to Have a Successful Freelance Education Career shares the options and practicalities of transitioning to and succeeding in a freelance career. Exploring options for both full-time and part-time freelancing, this essential guide outlines the key skills needed to build a stable career within the freelance education world.

Fe Luton explores ways to define and promote yourself and to make sure you stay top of the list when it comes to applications, commissions, and gigs. With chapters filled with practical advice, topics covered include:

- Life after (or alongside) teaching
- Developing skills beyond the classroom
- Pitching and making yourself stand out
- Building your online persona
- Career development
- The dos and don'ts of freelance work

This engaging yet highly practical guide is an essential read for anyone looking to reassess their options in the world of education and to expand their professional horizons beyond the classroom.

Fe Luton is a writer and trainer with over 25 years of experience working in the education sector as a teacher, key stage and subject lead, museum education officer, school governor, and researcher. She has developed and written teacher resources and articles for many years, and regularly contributes to an array of education publications. Alongside this, Fe also runs her own business, *Subject Leaders*, and currently works as a senior content writer for *We Are Futures*.

HOW TO HAVE A SUCCESSFUL FREELANCE EDUCATION CAREER

Stepping Outside the Classroom

Fe Luton

Routledge
Taylor & Francis Group

LONDON AND NEW YORK

Designed cover image: © Ascent/PKS Media Inc. / Getty Images

First published 2024
by Routledge
4 Park Square, Milton Park, Abingdon, Oxon OX14 4RN

and by Routledge
605 Third Avenue, New York, NY 10158

Routledge is an imprint of the Taylor & Francis Group, an informa business

© 2024 Fe Luton

British Library Cataloguing-in-Publication Data
A catalogue record for this book is available from the British Library

ISBN: 978-1-032-45709-3 (hbk)
ISBN: 978-1-032-45708-6 (pbk)
ISBN: 978-1-003-37833-4 (ebk)

DOI: 10.4324/9781003378334

Typeset in Interstate
by Apex CoVantage, LLC

For all my teacher friends.

CONTENTS

Preface   viii

1 Life after (or alongside) teaching – the options   1

2 Education jobs outside the classroom   7

3 Having a career plan   33

4 Skills beyond the classroom   41

5 So you want to go freelance ...   53

6 So you want a side hustle ...   63

7 The practicalities of freelance work   70

8 Pitching, prodding, and making yourself stand out   81

9 So you want to run your own business ...   91

10 Building your online persona   98

11 Shifting outside the classroom   107

12 The dos and don'ts of work beyond the classroom   112

PREFACE

I am often asked how I got into freelance education work, frequently by teachers desperate to make the leap from the classroom. My answer is usually "quite by accident", but the reality is that with some honest self-reflection, hard work, and a will to understand the education landscape, freelance education work is becoming a very real post-classroom career option.

I first fell into freelance work when I was working as a class teacher with middle-management responsibilities. A friend of my deputy head was looking for someone to write commercial English plans, and she thought I might fit the bill. From that I began pitching my ideas to education magazines, and after a foray into employed roles in museums and as a lead education researcher and writer, I became a fully-fledged, full-time freelancer.

I spent the next ten years learning to pitch, promote, and endear myself to a wide range of clients, while setting up my own company (Subject Leaders), with a teacher friend, along the way. I now find myself in a part-time employed role as a senior content writer for a social-impact agency, while I continue to enjoy working freelance gigs and running my business. This book came out of a passion for education and the acknowledgement that supporting teachers sometimes means helping them step beyond the classroom.

1 Life after (or alongside) teaching – the options

Living the dream . . .

When I explain to people what I do, they often gaze on wistfully and ask how I became a freelance education writer. The quick answer is that I built up grassroots education experience and dabbled in writing as a side hustle, before taking the plunge and leaving the profession (several times). The long answer is found in the pages of this book. The journey was very random, and I doubt I could replicate it. While it was an exciting ride, the reality was not always as perfect as the dream might suggest. I love what I do and had fun (and sweat and tears) getting here. I wouldn't change it and have no desire to leave the wider world of education any time soon. Once a teacher, always a teacher; but sometimes that teacher needs a change.

Finding your path

There is no hard and fast route into non-teaching education work, and each journey will be different for each individual, but I hope that I might be able to guide you along the way and broaden your mind to the opportunities out there, where to find them, and how to grab them.

The journey always begins in a classroom, though. If you want to work in the education world, nothing outdoes grassroots, school-based experience. Whether you have been teaching 3, 13, or 30 years, you will have something to bring to the table at a level that feels equivalent in responsibility, expertise, and (hopefully) pay. What's important, though, is to find the path that works for you and that feels sustainable, viable, and, above all, exciting.

Reasons for making the change

So often, when I talk to teachers about shifting beyond the boundaries of the classroom, they throw me the same reasons:

- I want to have a better work-life balance
- I feel like I'm always being judged
- I'm fed up with all the bureaucracy
- I don't feel appreciated
- I'm tired

DOI: 10.4324/9781003378334-1

Rarely do they tell me that it is because the job is not interesting, challenging, or fulfilling enough, or because they don't like the children; rather, these qualities tend to be precisely what we all love about the job: no two days are the same, the children are (generally) great, and the challenge and interest level of the job is high. It is crucial that we reflect on why we want to leave or shift our working patterns, and to look at the options without rose-tinted glasses. Sometimes a change of school or a change of pace (working part-time in teaching, for example) can actually help us recentre, but sometimes we do just need a change of direction. I hope to help guide you through the latter process over the next few chapters.

You need to be careful when looking for work opportunities outside of the classroom, not to suggest to potential employers that your teaching workload was too much (which it often is) and that you need a better work-life balance (which you usually do), as these are strong push factors rather than pull factors. Think carefully about why you want to leave teaching or why you want to add in a side hustle or reduce your teaching hours to take on a different part-time role, because pulls are far superior to pushes when it comes to long-term motivation and will help you stick with and enjoy new opportunities. I can guarantee that, if you do make a move, you will shift through moments when you look back and crave the ownership of your day, your room, a class full of charges, and the variety of work across each week. Some who leave submit to the pull back into the classroom, while others learn to rationalise their reasons for leaving and stick with it. For some people, time away from the classroom can reinvigorate a love for the profession and give them a new perspective on it, while for others, the longer they are away, the more convinced they are that they made the right decision.

Justifying any shift

You are likely to encounter suspicion around your reasons for "leaving the profession". You will need to be prepared to convince potential clients or employers that you won't easily up and skip back into the classroom; they may well have been stung before, as there certainly is a level of elasticity to leaving the classroom in its entirety. Although teaching is just another job to those of us working in the field, it is often seen from the outside as a vocation or calling, so people may question why you would want to leave the profession. The key is to be clear and positive about your reasons for any change.

Possible working patterns

In a shift away from the classroom, there are essentially five working-pattern options available to you, and reflecting on what works best for you is an important starting point. Consider that some options can lead to others: a side hustle could become a part-time split, which could become a whole new job or fully freelance opportunity. We'll explore further how these work in Chapter Three, but for now, let's reflect on the pros and cons of each.

Work pattern	Pros	Cons
A whole new job	• It is a clean slate, and if you want out fully, this is the route to take • Instant removal of any school stress (although there will still be stresses, just different ones)	• You're completely jumping ship, and while there is still a way back, this will be a big change • You'll have to find an employer willing to wait for you to work your notice period • Your overall earnings may go down
A part-time split	• You still get to stay in the classroom for part of the week • You will have 2-3 days outside of the classroom • Offers greater variety • Could ensure your overall earnings don't drop drastically • A great way to gently shift away from the classroom • Part-time freelance work will offer flexibility in your working week	• You are still in a classroom, which can feel like a drain if you don't want to be there • Your school work may intrude into working time that should be devoted to the new job • Could create conflicts of interest
A side hustle	• Great for building up skills and networks • A good way to dabble and see if you like working in a different field • Brings in money to supplement your salary	• Will add to your already busy workload • Could create conflicts of interest

(Continued)

(Continued)

Work pattern	Pros	Cons
Full-time freelance	• Offers a high degree of flexibility • Depending on the work, may increase your salary • Offers greater variety	• Potentially unreliable work • Securing enough work to fill your week can be stressful • No sick pay, pension, or holiday pay
Running your own business	• Offers a high degree of flexibility • You are your own boss • You can choose what you do	• May not bring any money in initially • Potentially stressful and long hours • No sick pay, pension, or holiday pay

All options are valid, and all options are possible, but make sure you take your time; don't undersell yourself or jump at the first thing that comes your way. Most of what we'll explore in this book focuses on the final three of these options - those freelance or self-employed paths. We will, however, also touch on salaried employment opportunities away from the classroom, where to find them, and how to approach them.

Can I earn the same salary?

While teaching may not always be perceived as an especially lucrative profession, once you have established your classroom career, shifting to another path brings with it the risk of a financial hit. The first shift I made away from teaching cost me a 30% salary drop, and after a dabble back into the classroom, the next departure cost me a 10% pay cut. The new jobs that I had shifted into were relatively well paid within their own sectors, and I was in the fortunate position that a pay cut was viable. This can often be the biggest barrier to shifting to work away from the classroom, but sometimes the other benefits can outweigh this loss, if the drop in pay is not a deal-breaker. Freelance work can be a more viable option for equivalent earnings, but, as we will see in Chapter Five, the money you earn as a freelancer is not always as clear-cut as it may seem.

What am I good at?

Before making any decisions, the first thing you need to do is identify who you are, what your skills and passions are, and what makes you unique or in-demand outside of the classroom. To achieve this, I like to employ a twist on the classic SWOT analysis: a SOAP analysis (Skills, Obstacles, Ambitions, Passions), which has a slightly more positive feel to it.

When I first took the plunge to go fully freelance (2013), it was driven by personal circumstances, as is often the case. At that time, my SOAP analysis (Figure 1.1) really helped direct me to the type of work I wanted to do and the kinds of organisations I wanted to work for.

Often employers, especially those without direct in-school experience, can struggle to see beyond your previous job title to notice the hidden, more granular details. Carrying out a SOAP analysis and picking out your skills is the first step to transforming your niche role in the classroom into a broader and more relatable list of skills. We will explore your transferable skills in greater depth in Chapter Four.

SKILLS (and experience)	OBSTACLES
Writing	Money
Research	Time
Training	Flexibility (*I had two very young*
Teaching	*children*)
Exhibition development	Where to go/who to approach/where
Museum education	to look
Creativity	

AMBITIONS	PASSIONS
To write a book (*this is my third!*)	Education
To have a flexible work pattern (*hard in*	Writing
2013, but lockdown has greatly helped	Research
with this)	Project work/planning
To be creative	Museums
To remain in education	Sport
To make a decent salary	Education politics
To have a good work-life balance	Reading
To be a famous actress (*still working on*	Movies
this one!)	Tech
To run my own business (have a look at	
Subject Leaders.co.uk)	

Figure 1.1 SOAP analysis for Fe Luton, 2013

Hit me with some options

There are lots of options for teachers in the non-classroom education world, and often they come packaged in a variety of ways, meaning that if you want a side hustle, some chunkier freelance work, a part-time shift, or a full-on plunge into the unknown, there are options out there for you. In the next chapter we explore some of these options and consider the experiences and skills you will need.

2 Education jobs outside the classroom

This is the chapter where you get to reflect on some of the options available to you as a teacher: options that use the skills, experience, and knowledge that you have built in the classroom and that are key to success in these roles. The skills that teachers bring with them to the workplace are hugely flexible and can find a home in many places. While emphasising that this is not a definitive list, we explore nine of the most common options, considering for each role:

- What it entails
- What the working options are
- What the pay is like
- Skills and qualifications that will help
- Additional experiences that will help
- Where to find these opportunities
- The pros and cons
- A case study

Each of these jobs have freelance and employment options. All of these jobs offer excellent opportunities for teachers to use and continue to use the skills they have built in the classroom. All potential earnings have been listed in comparison to the pay scales for teachers in England: Main Pay Range (MPR), Upper Pay Range (UPR), and Leadership Group Pay Range (LGPR).

Museum education

What is it?

Working in museums is many teachers' dream job. Being surrounded by interesting objects and getting to focus on educating without all of the stresses and pressures of the classroom sounds like the perfect option. Now, don't get me wrong: it truly is a great job. But having worked in two national museums and two local museums, I can attest that, while such work is highly fulfilling and uses your skills as a teacher to the maximum extent, there can be a lot of repetition involved in running the same school workshops over and over again. And when you don't have a teacher-pupil relationship with the children, behaviour management can be somewhat challenging.

DOI: 10.4324/9781003378334-2

The kinds of things you'll be doing may include:

- Writing resources – for school sessions
- Writing resources – for exhibitions
- Running school sessions
- Running outreach sessions in schools
- Running family workshops
- Running adult workshops
- Running Continuing Professional Development (CPD) sessions for teachers

Where can I find out more about museum education careers?

- The Group for Education in Museums (GEM): https://gem.org.uk/
- The Museums Association: www.museumsassociation.org/

Hours

- Freelance facilitators
- Part-time
- Full-time
- Some weekend hours

Pay

- Freelance day rate is often comparable to a day of supply teaching
- Salaries are comparable to MPR points 1–6, depending on the size of museum and seniority of the role

Where are jobs advertised?

- Museum websites
- The Group for Education in Museums (GEM): https://gem.org.uk/careers/job-search-results/
- The Museums Association: www.museumsassociation.org/careers/find-a-job/ (free registration required)
- National Museum Directors Council: www.nationalmuseums.org.uk/jobs/
- Museum Jobs: www.museumjobs.com/

Extra qualifications

- MA in museum studies will get you ahead and is sometimes listed among the preferred qualifications
- A relevant degree (e.g. history, anthropology, archaeology, art, or science)

Teaching skills that will help

- Classroom teacher experience
- Trips organisation (including risk assessments)
- Subject leadership (especially subjects of relevance, e.g. history, art, or science)
- Experience running in-school pupil workshops
- Experience running in-school CPD sessions for staff
- Resource creation

Additional experience that will help

- Voluntary work in the museums or galleries sector
- An active interest in museums or galleries

Pros

- You get to work in an amazing environment
- Paperwork is minimal
- No work to take home
- Much of the work can be enjoyable and creative
- You still get to touch base with children and young people

Cons

- Running school sessions or workshops can get repetitive
- You don't build a rapport with children and young people
- Hours can sometimes be unsociable
- You usually need to be on site
- It's a highly competitive field to break into

Case study

Museum education officer: Fe

Sometimes it is about being in the right place at the right time and other times it is about having the right experiences. My foray into the world of museum education started straight from my PGCE (Postgraduate Teaching Certificate in Education), when I got a summer job digging up fossil replicas in a purpose-built dinosaur dig on the grounds of the Natural History Museum. The work was very random and great fun, but the key for me was getting to know the education team and making contacts. After the summer, the museum kept me on in a freelance capacity, and then when a permanent job came up, I applied and got the role. This also got my ear to the ground in the other South Kensington museums, where I heard about a part-time freelance opportunity at the Victoria and Albert Museum. I worked between the two museums, topping up with some supply teaching for a few years before travelling and returning to the classroom. I also worked as an education officer at a local museum a few years later.

I really enjoyed the work and loved the environment, but I did find the school sessions quite repetitive and missed building a rapport with the children and young people I was interacting with. I loved running family and CPD workshops and greatly enjoyed the resource development, although my favourite part of the job was getting involved with exhibition development. The overall workload was very conducive to a good work-life balance and the general work benefits were favourable when working in a national or local-authority museum. The salary was comparable to teaching at that time, but since it has not increased over time in line with teaching salaries, it is now relatively lower.

Top tip: *Try to get some voluntary work experience in a local museum or look to get a foot in the door through freelance facilitator work.*

Education writing

What is it?

Writing for a living is a very broad and skill-specific career. As teachers, we are often in a good position to sidle into writing, either as a side hustle, a freelancer, or a fully employed writer. There are three main reasons why teachers find themselves in demand in this area:

1. **Specialist knowledge** – your subject specialism or general education knowledge are often in demand for content-writing roles with education publishers or publications
2. **Writing skills** – many teachers, especially those with an English studies background, are actually really good at writing. However, not all teachers are made equal when it comes to writing skills and the area is highly competitive
3. **Editorial skills** – most teachers mark work as part of their living. Primary and secondary teachers in subjects that require essay writing will have an edge in this. While you may not know the specifics of marking up a piece of writing in

terms of proofing or editorial guidelines, you will likely have an excellent eye for detail and an online course or training would bring you up to speed

There is a wide range of roles available across the field of writing:

- Content writing for commercial organisations
- Content writing for charities
- Teacher resources for education organisations, agencies, or quasi autonomous non-government organisations
- Article writing for education publishers
- Proofing with an education specialism
- Proofing across the board
- Content editing for education publishers
- Content editing across the board
- Creative writing - novels, poems, and short stories
- Non-fiction writing - textbooks or non-fiction books
- Specialist writing - phonics books or guidance
- Report writing with an education focus

Where can I find out more about writing careers?

ProCopywriters: www.procopywriters.co.uk/help-advice/
The Society of Authors: https://societyofauthors.org/Groups/Educational
National Association of Writers in Education (NAWE): www.nawe.co.uk/

Hours

- Freelance
- Part-time
- Full-time
- Often very flexible

Pay

- Freelance rates will need negotiation - sometimes it will be by the hour or day, at other times it will be by project or commission. Well-paid freelancers earn well over the equivalent daily supply rate
- Employed salaries are highly variable but are generally comparable to MPR points 1-6, depending on the organisation and seniority of role

Where are jobs advertised?

- **LinkedIn** - follow the organisations you feel your skills match, and keep an eye out for jobs. Search terms such as "education writer" or "education content writer" will throw up the right kinds of opportunities

- **Speculative approaches** – pitching for work is the key route into this kind of work, and you will often find that building up a freelance portfolio will allow you to go fully freelance or set you up better for a part-time or full-time employed role
- **Specific recruitment agencies** – DidTeach (www.didteach.com/) specialises in non-classroom roles for teachers or ex-teachers and often has writing roles. It is also worth keeping an eye on more general sites such as Workable (https://jobs.workable.com/) and Indeed (https://uk.indeed.com/) as well
- **Social Media** – follow organisations or companies that may fit your interests. Many individuals provide information about education jobs on their personal accounts, as well. For example, @Penny_ten has a weekly (Sunday morning) education jobs feed on her Twitter account

Extra qualifications

Any kind of writing course would help. There are many online short courses, but think carefully about what you want to develop before you start paying for courses:

- Copywriting/story-telling courses for more commercial writing and specialist education resource/article writing
- Copy editing or proofing courses for more editorial work
- Creative writing courses, if you are keen to dabble in works of fiction
- Journalism courses for writing articles for newspapers and education publications

Teaching skills that will help

- Writing experience (planning, policies, reports, newsletters etc)
- Evidence of creativity
- Resource development
- Subject (English) coordination or lead
- Moderation roles (for English)

Additional experience that will help

- Blog writing
- Voluntary print or web copywriting
- Writing in your free time

Pros

- Highly flexible
- Highly creative
- Uses your grassroots knowledge and skills
- Can be interesting, depending on the work
- Can be varied
- Hybrid or home working

Cons

- Can be quite pressured
- Commercial writing is very different from in-school writing, so you will need to develop skills much further
- Highly competitive
- Pay can be poor
- Work can be unreliable
- If freelance, you will need more than one "client"
- Can become repetitive/boring

Case studies

Content writer: Kate

I had been a primary teacher for around six years and was leading English, when I decided I needed a complete change. I left my full-time teaching role and took on short-term supply roles while I looked for a role in education writing. I picked up some freelance work, writing articles for various education publications before landing a role as an education content writer.

Resource developer: Chris

I was always interested in planning and resource development as a primary teacher and decided to approach some of the organisations whose planning and resources I used in the classroom to explore the options around working for them. Some were enthusiastic about my skills and creativity, while others either ignored me or offered payment that was just too low. After some dabbling on the side, I shifted into part-time teaching and part-time freelance resource development for an education charity.

> **Top tip:** *Craft your CV so that it presents your writing skills, then send out lots of speculative applications to organisations you'd like to do freelance work for. Make sure you have some examples of your own work to share.*

Education research

What is it?

Work in education research tends to take place in one of two types of setting: academic, i.e. universities and research institutes, and non-profit, i.e. education or social organisations (often charities) and think tanks. There are also opportunities to research in a more commercial context, but you may find you need sector experience for these roles. Research skills may be acquired academically, through a higher degree, or vocationally, through your work experience. Many teachers become involved in action research in school, which is a great route in; but also be aware that you are doing research on a regular basis for curriculum planning and sometimes for policy work. Teachers often have hidden, but very effective, research skills.

There are many different types of research-based work, including:

- Quantitative data research
- Qualitative research in schools or education settings
- Writing reports from primary research
- Writing reports from secondary research
- Running research programmes
- Evaluating in-school intervention or subject-specific programmes
- Government research
- Journalistic or education-landscape research

Where can I find out more about education research careers?

The Research Schools Network: https://researchschool.org.uk/
The National Foundation for Education Research (NFER): https://careers.nfer.ac.uk/NFER/Research

Hours

- Freelance
- Part-time
- Full-time
- The nature of research deadlines may require overtime here and there

Pay

- Freelance day rate often comparable to a day of supply teaching but can be greater depending on the organisation, need, and your expertise and skills. Rates may also be set per project rather than on a daily or hourly rate
- Salaries vary widely but are comparable to MPR points 1-6, depending on the type of contract and seniority of the role. Lead researchers and higher-up, academic roles are comparable to the UPR and LGPR. There is lots of scope for progression

Where are jobs advertised?

- Jobs.ac.uk: www.jobs.ac.uk/
- Times Higher Education jobs: www.timeshighereducation.com/unijobs/
- Charity Jobs often advertises education research roles: www.charityjob.co.uk/education-researcher-jobs
- Teacher-specific recruitment sites, LinkedIn, and social media (see afore-mentioned writing options)

Extra qualifications

- Masters-level degree in any subject that requires research is beneficial
- Masters-level degree or further studies in education
- Authorship of research-based studies that show you are trained in qualitative and quantitative research methods

Teaching skills that will help

- Action research in schools
- Subject leadership – especially where you have performed research for CPD, curriculum, policy documents, networking
- Development of in-school workshops or CPD
- Academic studies in your field
- Mentoring or tutoring trainee teachers

Additional experience that will help

- Publication of any research you have undertaken

Pros

- Hybrid or home working
- Work is interesting and can be cutting edge

- You see your work published and contributing towards the general good
- Some roles enable you to work with teachers, schools, and children
- Can lead to an academic role or a teacher-training role

Cons

- Can be very mentally challenging
- You may end up sitting at a desk all day
- Hours can be long when deadlines are looming
- Travel may be required
- On-site research work may be required

Case Study

Researcher: Noor

I had always been fascinated by action research and undertook several research projects through the research school I was teaching art at. I became so focused on research, that when an opportunity arose at a local university to get involved in some education research, I jumped at the chance. I continued to work part-time in schools while completing freelance research projects on the side. I am now enrolled for a PhD in education with a focus on the arts and academic development. I hope to shift into academic research once my studies are completed.

Top tip: *Speak to your headteacher, local authority, or academy trust to see if they are happy to support you in some action research in the classroom.*

Tutor

What is it?

Tutoring has become big business of late, especially post-lockdown, when not only are parents looking for private support for primary and secondary students in general, alongside GCSE/A-level tutoring, but schools are directly employing tutors to take small group work in schools. Traditionally, tutoring is something you organise yourself, privately, either by word-of-mouth or by advertising locally. However, tutoring companies have now become more commonplace, especially in areas where 11+ tutoring is sought after or for schools where common entrance exams are implemented. With the right networks, experience, knowledge, and confidence, tutoring can be very lucrative.

These days tutoring can be face-to-face or online, with a range of options available:

- Private group tutoring (often through a tutoring company)
- Private one-to-one tutoring
- Exam-specific tutoring: SATs, 11-plus, Common Entrance, GCSEs, A-levels
- In-school group or individual tutoring

Where can I find out more about tutoring careers?

Contact local schools and tutoring organisations to find out what experience they expect their tutors to have and what the work will look like.

Hours

- Freelance
- Part-time
- Full-time possible, but may need to be a mix of tutoring types and will require some evening and weekend hours
- School holidays will require different work patterns

Pay

- Freelance hourly rate can range depending on the nature of the tutoring and the expertise of the tutor. These will usually be comparable to MPR and UPR pay scale daily rates
- The day rate for in-school tutoring is comparable to a day of supply teaching, depending on the expected qualifications and experience
- Salaries from tutoring companies will vary according to need and client – some will offer term-time only contracts, while others will offer year-round contracts

Where are jobs advertised?

Tutoring jobs by their nature tend to be local jobs, although online tutoring has broadened this scope. As such, you will need to look at local social media outlets and approach local tutoring companies for vacancies. For online tutoring options, there are a huge range of companies that advertise posts; use the search term "online tutor jobs" to explore the huge range of opportunities.

Extra qualifications

- A subject-specific degree
- Courses or qualifications for specific interventions

- CPD from school with a focus on subjects you will tutor in or specific learning needs you will support

Teaching skills that will help

- The more teaching experience you have, the better
- Prior experience of any one-to-one or in-school tutoring work
- Teaching in key year groups or phases (e.g. Years 2 and 6 for primary SATs/11-plus or GCSE/A-level teaching)
- Prior "success" in tutoring
- Leading in a SENCo role or lead for "high attaining" pupils

Pros

- You will likely have time during the school day to work elsewhere, if this is an option for you
- Paperwork is minimal
- You still help children and young people progress, but without the pressures of the classroom
- Hourly pay is good
- Some roles enable you to work with teachers and pupils in school

Cons

- One-to-one tutoring can be tiring and intense
- Usually you'll need to be on-site at a school, a tutoring business, or a tutee's home
- Lesson planning still needs to be fitted in around tutor hours and factored into pay
- Work tends to be freelance, although there may be employment opportunities via tutoring businesses
- Hours need to fit in around the school day and/or around your teaching hours, if you are still working in the classroom
- Some weekend and evening work is likely
- Can be very stressful when parents are expecting a specific outcome (e.g. a pass or a specific grade)

Case study

Personal and school-based tutor: Alice

I have always topped up my part-time teaching salary through one-to-one tutoring. The pay rate is good and I enjoy the working relationship

I've built with my tutees. I greatly enjoy watching their progression and increasing confidence and now that I have more experience teaching in Year 6, I have taken on more tutees requiring SATs and 11+ support. I have recently shifted my working week so that I do three days in the classroom and have a day a week at a different school, where I have a one-to-one tutoring role, supporting pupils with maths and English. The fifth day is made up of my out of school tutoring, which I find doesn't add as much to my workload as the extra teaching days would, but still gives me the buzz (and salary) that comes with teaching.

Top tip: *Build up your tutees gradually so that you know where the sweet spot is in terms of your capacity.*

Outdoor education

What is it?

Working in outdoor education can be very good for the soul. With the increase in popularity of Forest Schools, Beach Schools, and school gardening, this has become a more in-demand area. Many roles, such as running school sessions or workshops, are freelance, but some contracted opportunities, such as running forest schools and the like, are also available. Outdoor activity centres often employ education specialists to run secondary fieldtrips for geography and environmental science, while others prefer to employ teachers to run school sessions. When in an employed role, you will often be involved in the development of resources and content as well as activity development and implementation.

Outdoor education has a broad remit, and you may find yourself involved in a range of activities:

- Running school sessions/workshops
- Developing activities and resources
- Running outreach sessions in schools
- Running field studies programmes
- Running adult education
- Running corporate events

Where can I find out more about outdoor education careers?

- Council for Learning Outside the Classroom: www.lotc.org.uk/category/jobs/
- Learning through Landscapes: https://ltl.org.uk/
- Institute for Outdoor Learning: www.outdoor-learning.org/

Hours

- Freelance facilitators
- Part-time
- Full-time
- Some weekend hours

Pay

- Freelance day rates can be comparable to a day of supply teaching but depend on the organisation, need, and your expertise, specific skills, and qualifications. You may also find yourself on seasonal contracts, meaning you will need additional sources of income to ensure year-round earnings
- Salaries vary widely but can be comparable to MPR points 1-4, depending on the type of contract and seniority of the role. Entry level roles are often well below the MPR

Where are jobs advertised?

- Countryside Jobs: www.countrysidejobslink.co.uk/
- Council for Learning Outside the Classroom: www.lotc.org.uk/category/jobs/
- Teacher-specific recruitment sites, LinkedIn, and social media (see aforementioned writing options)

Extra qualifications

- Outdoor education training
- Learning Through Landscapes qualifications
- Qualified Forest School or Beach School practitioner
- Subject-specific qualifications (e.g. degree in environmental science, geography etc)

Teaching skills that will help

- Facilitating outdoor learning sessions in school
- Sustainability lead or eco-schools lead
- Geography, history, or science subject specialisation or lead
- Running clubs with an outdoor theme (gardening/nature/eco club)
- Forest or Beach School lead

Additional experience that will help

- Volunteering for outdoors or environmental organisations
- Being a keen gardener
- Being an outdoor-pursuits enthusiast
- Volunteering for children's organisations with a focus on the outdoors (e.g. Scouts, Guides Woodland Folk etc)

Pros

- You get to work outside (see also cons!)
- Paperwork is minimal
- Some roles enable you to work with teachers, schools, and children
- Much of the work can be enjoyable and creative

Cons

- Working outside can be cold and wet or very hot
- Can get repetitive
- You don't build a rapport with children unless it is a repeat session
- Hours can include weekend work
- You need to be on site
- Highly competitive
- Work may be seasonal

Case study

Forest School practitioner and outdoor learning specialist: Niamh

I spent 12 years working in early years education, during which time I trained as a Forest School practitioner. I then worked as a freelance practitioner for the local woodland trust before becoming a part-time member of staff. I found this opened up lots of freelance opportunities to develop environmental teaching resources and CPD programmes for schools, and now spend half my week working freelance and the rest running schools programmes.

Top tip: consider a range of options that use your skills so that you are not spending the entire week outside - it can get very cold and wet in the winter!

Extracurricular clubs

What is it?

Clubs are very much in demand these days, whether they are connected to specific schools or run privately in local community centres or spaces. As hybrid ways of working have resulted in parents taking on more flexible hours, sending children to clubs is often seen as a great substitute for childcare. Big hitters tend to be languages, the arts, sports, and anything outdoorsy or with an eco-edge. Teachers hold a lot of appeal when they run a club – parents feel like they are paying for high quality.

If this is an option that appeals, there are plenty of flexible approaches:

- Workshops
- A weekly club in schools (lunchtime or before/after school)
- Holiday workshop sessions
- Outreach sessions to schools
- CPD
- In-school support

Where can I find out more about careers running clubs?

- Out of School Alliance: https://outofschoolalliance.co.uk/activity-clubs

Hours

- Freelance facilitators
- Part-time
- Some weekend hours
- School holidays may affect your hours

Pay

- Hourly rate can be quite high, depending on the popularity of the club, but you do need to factor in any preparation time or materials that you have paid for, and the fact that you may only be running a few clubs a week

- Tends not to be salaried, so you may need a top-up income

Where are jobs advertised?

- There are several club franchises you can buy into where you get support, guidance, and marketing, but they will also take a cut of your earnings. Contract sign-ins may also make going it alone tricky after the event: www.franchise-uk.co.uk/language/
- Usually you will be creating your own club and will need to ramp up local interest yourself

Extra qualifications

- Anything that connects to your club (e.g. a degree in art/practising artist; qualified sports coach; Level 3 in horticulture etc)

Teaching skills that will help

- School club organisation
- Trips organisation
- Subject leadership
- In-school workshops

Additional experience that will help

- Working with children in a non-school setting
- Social media and marketing experience

Pros

- You get to focus on a topic area you love
- You get to be your own boss
- You build a rapport with children who regularly attend your club
- You are not restricted by curriculum expectations

Cons

- Paperwork can be complex (insurances/permissions etc)
- Hours can be unsociable
- You need to be on site
- You will need to market it yourself
- If you miss a week, or if a session has to be cancelled, you don't earn any money

Case study

Art club lead: Mo

I loved being an art teacher but had reached a point where I wanted more flexibility in my work, as I had a young family at home. I also wanted to focus fully on my specialist area and have time to practise art, so I started running regular weekly art clubs in the early evening for secondary age children and on Saturdays and Sundays for primary age children. I now also run a drop-in art session for pre-schoolers and their carers during the weekday mornings. During the school holidays I run whole morning or whole afternoon workshops. I love being in full control of what is essentially still teaching, and love seeing the growth in confidence and skill in my regular attendees.

It can get tricky when I want to go away for a weekend, and I need to rely on family to help with weekend childcare. It has also allowed me the time to practise my own art and I have started exhibiting and taking commissions, which offers me another income stream.

Top tip: *try to maximise the number of regular clubs you run to help maintain a steady and loyal audience and income. Either ask for payment for blocks of weeks or ensure it is paid a week in advance.*

Education officer

What is it?

Working as an education officer essentially means being in charge of the education arm of an organisation, setting, or company. The role itself varies hugely but could include:

- Running school sessions on site or in school settings
- Writing web-based education content, including blogging
- Creating education resources or plans for teachers to use in class, or on site if you are at a heritage site
- Organising volunteers to run in-school programmes
- Overseeing work experience
- Knowledge and information management
- Running CPD
- Project/programme management

Education officers also work for local authorities or Multi-Academy Trusts (MATs), using their specialist knowledge and experience to support schools in implementing effective education initiatives. You will need to be fairly versatile and up for any challenge that comes your way.

Where can I find out more about education officer careers?

- Local authority education officer careers: www.inputyouth.co.uk/jobguides/job-educationofficerlocalauthority.html

Hours

- Freelance commissions for resource development
- Part-time

- Full-time
- Occasionally evening and weekend hours, depending on the organisation

Pay

- Salaries are comparable to MPR points 1-6, depending on size and nature of organisation. Senior roles tend not to attract high salaries, but shifting towards a "head of education" or "director of education" can shift salaries towards an UPR equivalent in certain organisations. Local-authority education officer jobs attract a higher salary.

Where are jobs advertised?

- **LinkedIn** - follow the organisations you feel your skills match, and keep an eye out for jobs. Search terms such as "education officer" or "learning officer" will throw up the right kinds of opportunities
- **Specific recruitment agencies** - DidTeach (www.didteach.com/) specialises in non-classroom roles for teachers or ex-teachers and often has education officer roles. It is also worth keeping an eye on more general sites such as Workable (https://jobs.workable.com/) and Indeed (https://uk.indeed.com/)
- **Twitter/FaceBook/social media** - follow organisations or companies that may fit your interests
- **JobsGoPublic or local-authority jobs pages** - education officer jobs within local authorities or public-sector organisations tend to advertise on their own jobs boards and www.jobsgopublic.com
- **TES, EducationWeek jobs, or national press** - roles in MATs will tend to be advertised on general education jobs boards as well as their own websites

Extra qualifications

- Any qualifications that link into the organisation's focus would help
- Subject or specific key stage experience for local-authority or MAT education officer roles
- Project management

Teaching skills that will help

- Trips organisation
- Subject leadership
- Senior leadership
- Running in-school workshops and CPD
- Writing experience (planning, resources, policies, reports etc)

Additional experience that will help

- Voluntary work in the sector
- Publication of relevant resources or articles

Pros

- Highly creative
- Uses your grassroots knowledge and skills
- Uses any expertise you have
- Can be interesting, depending on the work
- Can be varied
- Pay can be good in local-authority and MAT roles
- Can be an organisation you feel you want to get behind

Cons

- Can get be quite pressured
- Highly competitive
- Pay can be poor in the general sector
- Can become repetitive/boring

Case study

Education officer: Stella

I spent seven years working in a local primary school, leading on English and Early Years, before taking on some support work for my local authority, where I ran CPD for local teachers. I shifted into freelance supply teaching while I looked for an education role outside of the classroom, ultimately moving into an education officer role at a national reading charity part-time, while continuing to run CPD for my local authority. I love how I have been able to specialise in English and reading and enjoy supporting schools to implement effective and exciting projects and programmes. While I miss being in the classroom, I still feel my work is having a positive impact on pupils.

Top tip: *if you are keen to shift from your classroom role, taking on supply teaching roles is a great (and relatively safe) step to take, while you are looking for work.*

School librarian

What is it?

Working as a school librarian has a lot of appeal if books are your thing. Not only do you get to while away the hours in a room full of books, but you also don't lose the connection with young people and education. Some school librarian roles require full librarian qualifications while others focus more on experience in schools and a willingness to learn.

School librarians have a range of responsibilities:

- Classic librarian book-management tasks
- Staff CPD
- Student CPD
- Research support
- Networking with exam boards (secondary), authors, publishing houses
- Resource and activity guide writing
- Library lessons/workshops
- Library club

Where can I find out more about school librarian careers?

The Chartered Institute of Library and Information Professionals (CILIP): www.cilip.org.uk/page/JobsandCareers

Hours

- Occasionally freelance
- Part-time
- Full-time
- May be term-time only contracts

Pay

- Some salaries are comparable to MPR points 1–4, depending on size of the school and library and the duties expected, but starting salaries can be below this. The salary rarely enters the upper levels of the MPR.

Where are jobs advertised?

- TES, Schools Week, local-authority job boards
- CILIP jobs board: https://informationprofessionaljobs.com/cilip-hq-job/

Extra qualifications

- A post-graduate library qualification

Teaching skills that will help

- Subject leadership/any management skills
- Writing experience (planning, policies, reports etc)
- Running library clubs
- Helping out with school libraries
- Knowledge of reading-education techniques and awareness of current fiction trends/releases

Additional experience that will help

- Blogging about books
- Volunteering in your local library

Pros

- Uses your grassroots knowledge and skills in a non-classroom setting
- Can be interesting if you are into books
- Can be varied
- Allows you to build a rapport with pupils

Cons

- Highly competitive
- Pay can be poor
- Can become repetitive and boring
- Contracts may be term-time only

Case study

School librarian: Holly

I had been working part-time, long-term supply at a local school when they asked if I would run a library club. When the current English lead suggested that I took over her role running the library, I jumped at it. Initially it was a freelance role, usually a morning a week, but became a rolling term-time contract once I started running library classes for pupils across the school (essentially, I became PPA cover!). I now work every morning in the library and do my own freelance writing work at home in the afternoons or do extra supply work at my school.

Top tip: try to build your skills while in a teaching role, so that you have specific in-school librarian experiences. Volunteering at your local library will add great value into this experience.

Consultancy

What is it?

Becoming an education consultant is a great way to exercise your experience and knowledge in whatever way you like - freelance, part-time, or full-time, employed or running your own business. The only caveat is that you need a lot of experience and need to have something tangible, and possibly unique, to offer. You will have been in senior management and will have an "area" of expertise, such as:

- **School improvement** - you may have extensive experience in turning a school or department around into an outstanding provision
- **Subject specialism** - you have lived and breathed your subject for years and know what looks good and how to succeed in creating an effective department
- **Curriculum specialist** - you have spent years developing and crafting curriculums and may have been a director of studies
- **Safeguarding specialist** - extra qualifications, senior roles, and a vast amount of experience mean you can inject confidence into schools in this tricky area
- **Wellbeing specialist** - you may have been a wellbeing lead for pupils and/or staff. Possibly, you have additional qualifications linking to wellbeing
- **EdTech specialist** - you may have been a computing lead and have extensive experience of implementing edtech across the curriculum. Experience with tech-based school systems and apps makes you an expert in your field

Some key functions of a consultancy role may include:

- Advising
- Developing policies
- Supporting teachers
- Supporting senior leaders
- Developing action plans
- Running CPD

- Writing articles
- Writing books

Hours

- Freelance
- Part-time
- Full-time
- Often very flexible hours

Pay

- Freelance rates will need negotiation – sometimes it will be by the hour or day; other times it will be by project or consultancy period. Consultants can charge whatever they like, but rates generally tend to be somewhere between two and five times a daily supply teaching rate
- Employed salaries are generally comparable to UPR and GLPR, depending on the organisation and seniority of role

Where are jobs advertised?

LinkedIn – follow the organisations you feel your skills match and keep an eye out for jobs. Search terms such as "education consultant" or "special-ist" with your specific strengths and experiences (e.g. "school improve-ment specialist") will turn up the right kinds of opportunities.

Speculative approaches – approaching organisations (e.g. Osiris), schools, MATs, or local authorities directly is a key route into this kind of work. You will find that building up a consultancy portfolio will allow you to build a reputation.

Networking – building and using networks is important. The more you are known and respected, the greater the network and likelihood of recom-mendation or head-hunting.

Consultant agencies – The Society of Education Consultants (www.sec.org.uk/) holds a wide range of consultants on its books and is a go-to plat-form for many looking for consultancy work.

Extra qualifications

- MA in education
- Headteacher qualification
- Subject-specific master's degree
- Vocational training or qualifications

Teaching skills that will help

- Writing experience (planning, policies, reports etc)
- Senior management
- Work in a variety of school settings
- Working in schools to help improve outcomes
- Advisory roles
- Mentoring roles
- Experience running CPD
- Involvement in Initial Teach Training

Additional experience that will help

- Consultancy across other schools
- Networking skills

Pros

- Highly flexible
- Uses your expert knowledge and skills
- Can be interesting depending on the work
- Can be varied
- Excellent pay
- Opportunity to work across a range of schools and settings
- No direct in-school senior responsibilities

Cons

- Can be very pressured, with high expectations
- It is very different from in-school work, and while you build relationships with staff and pupils, these are not long-term
- Quite competitive
- Work can be unreliable
- If freelance, you will need more than one "client"

Case study

School improvement consultant - Ben

I started my career as a geography teacher, soon moving to head of geography, deputy head, then headteacher. I was always striving to achieve high standards, support school improvement and push for better outcomes for pupils, so when I left teaching it was a natural fit to become a freelance education consultant for school improvement and curriculum development. I now work in a hybrid way, employed part-time as a curriculum lead in a MAT, Monday to Wednesday, and a freelance consultant on Thursdays and Fridays. The variety really suits me and I have lots of flexibility with my freelance work, while enjoying the benefits of a regular salary.

Top tip: as you build experience in school, try to find a niche area to specialise in and work hard to be the go-to person for that in your school. Offer out your expertise to other local or trust schools to build your reputation from within the profession.

So, as you can see, there are plenty of options. And we have only covered some of them here. There are also, for example, a multitude of opportunities within the EdTech industry and within commercial learning and development departments. Teachers' skills and expertise are certainly in demand, and a range of opportunities are available if you look in the right places. In the next chapter, we start to consider how to develop a career plan that works for you.

3 Having a career plan

So, you've decided on a change or a shift into new opportunities, and you've considered some of the possible options. What is the next step? Teaching may be highly challenging as a profession, but we certainly can't fault it for continually striving to improve or develop its teachers, nor for offering a clear range of career trajectories. When it comes to non-teaching opportunities, however, the CPD we once relied on to support, develop, or redirect our careers is less readily available, and you may find yourself scrambling around looking for tangible career trajectories. For this reason, teachers need to think beyond "I need out" and taking any job that will get them there, or they will inevitably regret the move. Yes, by all means, jump ship to do something completely different, but make sure you do so with a plan.

What's your five- to ten-year plan?

It is a bit of a cliché, but knowing what the ultimate plan is can help enormously as you make decisions and build skills. Whether you are building skills within teaching but with an exit plan, or jumping ship for a new life, you need to see the path ahead. Where do you hope to be in ten years' time, and how do you hope to get there? When looking for new opportunities, be clear about longer-term opportunities for promotion and career development. This is easier to do when you are looking for an employed alternative to teaching than when operating in a freelance context, in which it is quite hard to envision the next five or ten years, simply because the next steps are not necessarily obvious. You might want to be running your own business or be in an employed role by then, or simply to have diversified your clients and skills as a fully-fledged freelancer.

Whatever your aims, it's important to carefully consider the skills development, training, and learning you will seek along the way, and not to lose sight of a career trajectory. It is also important to give careful consideration to the overarching approach you'd like to take to begin this journey. Which of the following plans best describes you?

Plan A: the side hustler

You want a side hustle because you'd like eventually to shift out of the classroom or to teach part-time

Side hustles are a great way to expand your skill set and broaden your networks and experiences. Many employers outside of teaching who want to hire

DOI: 10.4324/9781003378334-3

ex-teachers are often looking for something in addition to classroom experience, or at the very least are drawn to someone who has extra skills that will make them stand out.

1. **Set out a roadmap**: is there a specific skill set or job role that you have in mind that you would like to develop or break into? Writing? Training? Running outdoor eco workshops? Think about the kinds of job or business opportunity you'd like to pursue and consider the skills and experiences that would help
2. **Have a training plan**: identify the skills or experiences you want to build, and find ways to develop them. This could be through free online courses from organisations such as FutureLearn,[1] or through your own research, face-to-face courses, or online videos
3. **Give yourself a timescale**: you may decide to start paring back your teaching, or shift to more supply teaching, so that you can start to develop your skill set and opportunities away from the classroom. But give yourself a timescale for this – one that works financially, mentally, and emotionally

Plan B: the freelancer

You are taking the plunge and going freelance, or have decided to start your own business

This is generally the boldest and hardest of the moves, but it can also be very rewarding. It also happens to be the route where you most commonly feel you are not progressing.

1. **Again with the roadmap**: it is easy to lose track of your goals in the fully freelance world, so it is really important to set this out
2. **Plan for CPD**: you will have to pay for it and lose work hours to complete it – a double blow, but one that needs to be absorbed into your costs. Whether it's courses, meetings, networking, or conferences, make sure you keep up with what is going on in your new area and develop the skills you need to keep moving forward
3. **Plan to retrain**: you may want to retrain in your new chosen area; for example, if you decide to become a writer, you may wish to complete a writing course on the side, or you may wish to complete a vocational course (speech therapy, paediatric nursing, library qualification) while you supply teach
4. **Update your CV**: make sure you update your CV to reflect the freelance work you want to do. Having a CV that reflects your skills repackaged away from teaching makes pitching for work much easier and draws clients away from just seeing the teacher in you

Plan C: the get me out of here now-er

You are actively looking for a different job

If you are proactively looking for an employed role outside of teaching that matches your current salary, it will likely be in the education world. You'll need to take a considered approach to ensure you continue to grow and thrive.

1. **The roadmap still stands**: whichever way you are shooting, remember that this is the next step in your career; so make sure it keeps you travelling. Is this next step your end-game or is it a stepping-stone to something else? How can you train or develop to shift up and along in your chosen path?
2. **Consider the CPD available**: know that you may need to find it for yourself. What will help you in your new role, and what will help move you forwards from here?
3. **Plan for change**: consider if there is anything you can do to prepare yourself for the shift in work pattern. Will you suddenly be sat at a desk all day? Will you be expected to interact more with other adults and clients?
4. **Create a non-teaching CV**: having a CV that reflects your skills repackaged away from teaching makes job applications much clearer and draws clients away from just seeing the teacher in you

Try before you buy

Whichever category you come under, sticking your toe into uncharted waters can feel like a big risk. One of the options available to you is to get some good, old-fashioned work experience during the school holidays. This way you can get a realistic feel, from an insider's point-of-view, for how your career could develop. Such experience will not only give you a better understanding of the consequences of your potential shift, but also provide a new set of networks and contacts.

- **Contact companies or departments directly:** people love sharing their work with others, and love even more sharing their workload. If you can set out clearly what your rationale is for the work experience, and even suggest to them what jobs you could do while there, you'd be surprised how many will fall over themselves to welcome you in
- **Think about your immediate networks and contacts:** do you know anyone who may be able to help out? Do you have friends or family with connections? Approaching organisations through contacts makes you more of a known quantity

- **Consider more distant contacts**: are you on LinkedIn[2]? See if any of your connections work for or have their own connections with people who can help. Seek out people in the organisations you are looking for and see if they will "connect in" with you
- **Offer to run sessions in a voluntary capacity**: offering to take some sessions in a local museum, woodland trust, or library will give you a feel for what this kind of work entails. It is very different from teaching in a classroom: you have less of a personal relationship; often adults you don't know are watching; you'll be managing lots of different ages and stages; you'll be outside of the classroom environment; and there will be a lot of repetition. If you are thinking of running clubs in the community – art clubs, gardening clubs etc – or considering a move to museum education or outdoor education, having a go first will help you think about how to organise it and determine whether you actually like it

Travelling forwards

Once you have identified your path and set out your plan, make sure you continue to champion your development by reflecting on your progress, setting new goals, and developing new skills.

Annual reviews

There is something nice about knowing that, as a freelancer, you don't have to take part in the paperwork carnival that surrounds an annual review. However, it is very easy for the years to slip by without really reflecting on your personal development and goals for the future. If you are not in direct employment but work freelance in some capacity, or run your own business, make sure you perform an annual review of yourself (you can use the questions in Appendix 1), reflecting on your achievements, wins, and areas for development. Make sure you set out your aims and goals for the ensuing 12 months and identify ways of achieving them. If possible, find a close friend, family member, or ex-colleague who can go through your review with you; getting an outsider's perspective can really help. Make sure you identify skills and experiences that are building blocks and those that are completely new; this will help you to see how you are using and building prior skill sets, but also where you have grown over the past year.

A great exercise to do each year in your "annual review" is to update your CV. Add in new skills and experiences and keep a written statement about why you are great at your current role, adding in each year's experiences. Not only does this help you to reflect on your development, but it also means that if you do decide to make a move or shift into paid employment, your credentials are up to scratch.

Continuing Professional Development (CPD)

CPD doesn't always have to be a course; it can be skills development through other means. Consider the following options for professional development.

Develop broader education knowledge

- Write a blog – commit to writing on education issues
- Follow education journalists online
- Sign up to updates from education establishments and organisations of relevance and read the emails that land in your inbox from them

Develop writing skills

- You already do writing – of plans, curriculum, newsletters, reports, letters home – so continue to find other opportunities to write in school
- Start a blog about something that interests you
- Try writing articles for education publications
- Consider both fiction and non-fiction writing (the latter is easier to break into)

Develop project management skills

- Reflect on the skills that you already have – running programmes, year groups, class trips etc
- Start to use project-management systems where appropriate and possible. Many offer free trials to give you a flavour of what they entail
- Manage any side hustle with a "project-management" approach
- Complete training on project management, from, for example, FutureLearn or The Association for Project Management[3]

Develop EdTech skills

- Join in free courses, webinars, and conferences – EdTech is a booming area and there is a lot out there to benefit from
- Push outside your comfort zone in your current role to explore and experiment with EdTech
- Try out a wide range of EdTech tools in class to get a feel for what works well and what doesn't

Develop personnel and people skills

- Offer to run CPD and staff meetings
- Do you line-manage anyone? If this is something you are keen to do, your head may be open to you line-managing teaching assistants or less experienced members of the teaching staff
- Consider any student teacher or Early Career Teacher (ECT) mentoring you have done or would like to do
- Consider the parent-management skills that you already have – parents are essentially clients in the private sector

When the plan doesn't work – returning to teaching

If your plan doesn't work, you may decide on a return to the classroom, and, in fact, having had some time away might be just what you needed. Do be aware, though, that the longer you are out of the classroom, the harder it will be to slip back in:

First year out: let's face it – this is essentially a sabbatical, and you could very much present it as such in any campaign to return to the classroom.

Two-three years out: this is a career break, but, to be honest, if you have kept your hand in and actually know what the reality of the classroom still is, then, again, the time out is not really a problem, especially if you have been doing something "in education" that you can argue will enhance your classroom practise or that helps you to stand out, or if you have continued to supply-teach.

Four-six years: returning is getting a bit harder now, but by no means is it impossible. Plenty of people take time out of a teaching career for an array of reasons, both personal and professional. But you do need to be cognisant of potential issues at this point:

1 Are you really up to scratch with the realities of the current classroom? If you have kept up with the education profession in your time away, you will know the implications of any changes, but be aware of how quickly trends in pedagogy and language develop, and how approaches to planning and teaching change. You'll also need to be aware of any curriculum updates or new subject guidance which may have come into effect while you have been out of the classroom

2 The pay. Pay is always a consideration when we leave the classroom, but, in fact, there can also be a pay problem if you decide to return. You will be asked where you were on the pay scale when you left and then be promptly popped straight back there if you join a local authority

(LA) school. Trust me: it has happened to me. Academies and independent schools will be more willing to negotiate and far more open to your experiences outside of the classroom, but, generally, an LA head's hands are completely tied when it comes to pay scales, unless you have recent teaching payslips to back up your salary request

Seven-plus years: we need to be realistic at this point, as schools are unlikely to bring you in unless you have been up to something spectacularly relevant for the past seven years, or, if you are lucky, if recruiting teachers has become particularly challenging and schools are very open to employing "returners" to the profession. There will be an element of employer nervousness about whether you will stay, especially if employers feel that the landscape has changed dramatically since you were last in a classroom, or that conditions have gone so far downhill that you will run at the first sign of trouble. Remember, by this stage, you have a whole new career as a back-up, and schools will know that you can return to that if you so wish. As the years have gone by, my belief in my alternative education career has grown, and it is only now, ten years on from my last classroom gig, that I know I won't return – mainly because they probably wouldn't have me, but also because I now believe that I have a fully-fledged career outside the classroom.

In the next chapter we begin to look at ways to develop, highlight, and capitalise upon your niche knowledge and experience.

Appendix 1

Annual review

Consider the following questions on an annual basis to ensure your career continues to move forwards:

1. What have you achieved in the past 12 months that you are proud of?
2. What new skills have you developed?
3. What new experiences have you had?
4. Have you achieved any new streams of work?
5. What have you enjoyed the most in the past 12 months?
6. What have you found frustrating or disliked in the past 12 months?
7. What would make your job easier to do?
8. How have you managed your workload and "clients" in the past 12 months?
9. How has your work-life balance been in the past 12 months?
10. What would you like to aim for or achieve in the next 12 months?
11. What new skills are you keen to develop?
12. Are there any CPD courses you'd like to complete?

Set yourself three key targets to aim for in the next 12 months. These will set you up for your next annual review.

Notes

1   www.futurelearn.com/.
2   www.linkedin.com/.
3   www.apm.org.uk/qualifications-and-training/.

4 Skills beyond the classroom

When we start looking at earning options outside of the classroom, it can sometimes feel like a stretch to see beyond our teaching skills. And potential employers or clients can also be blind to the remarkable number of broad and transferable skills teachers have, seeing only a packaged "teacher". To be successful outside of teaching, you are going to need to identify the specific skills you have, what you are stand-out good at, and how you can prove it. You'll need to unwrap your teacher packaging so that you can pick apart the individual skills. Organisations often want the experience of a teacher but not an actual teacher; it's a subtle but important difference.

Teachers, by their nature, are creative creatures. We take a fairly bland curriculum and make it fun, engaging, and exciting for our pupils, trying to instil a sense of fascination and a desire to learn. When you think about a shift from the classroom, you need to shift that creativity into a different space – somewhere you can remain creative but in a way that fits a different remit.

Transferable skills

I have always been told that teachers have an excellent haul of transferable skills, which sounds good, in theory. But the reality is that we need to dig deep and tease out what these skills are and to frame them in a way that the non-teaching world can understand and embrace. Essentially, you need to break down the day-to-day tasks you do and then translate them into non-classroom skills. Think about the kinds of things you might do in any 24-hour period:

- Writing
- Performing or presenting
- Communicating
- Running assemblies or staff meetings
- Planning lessons
- Managing conflicts
- Managing and overseeing other staff
- Managing projects
- Implementing effective time management
- Offering creative solutions to problems

DOI: 10.4324/9781003378334-4

- Dealing with and managing parents
- Organising large groups of pupils

The list could go on. But what do these equate to in the real world? It's hard to know where to begin. And therein lies the greatest problem teachers face with their transferable skills. Do we end up a Jack-of-all-trades but master of none? It can sometimes feel that way. But if we break down what we do and repackage it for the non-teaching world, our skills begin to feel far more open and malleable.

Let's explore some of these skills and where they are evidenced:

Writing

If you are a primary teacher or secondary English teacher, you not only teach writing but also write in a variety of styles and formats: reports, planning documents, letters, policy statements ... the list goes on.

Design

You already create your own resources, which will likely be creative and well-designed. You know your audience and understand the kind of design that translates into effective engagement and learning.

Strategy

Everything you do takes objectives and transforms them into a learning programme. Your short-, medium-, and long-term plans are all forms of strategy, as is any policy- or programme-development you are involved in.

Communication

You are an excellent communicator:

- Verbal communication on a one-to-one basis; with groups, whole classes, and schools; in staff meetings; and with parents
- Written communication (audiences) – you can write effectively for children, teachers, senior leaders, external organisations, and parents
- Written communication (forms) – you communicate in a variety of forms, including reports, plans, letters, and policies

Project management

You do this within and beyond the school grounds. Think about all the trips, celebration events, in-school class events, and whole school social events you have managed.

Your day-to-day job is also one big project-management task – think of all the planning you do and the constant need for adaptation and flexibility this demands.

Acting/performance

You effectively do this on a daily basis. Knowing what you are going to say to hold an audience (and a very tricky one at that) is a form of performance. You also do it when you run assemblies or even when you "show" a class your breaking point, even though they'd actually have to push a lot further! The younger the age group you teach, the more likely you have honed these creative skills.

Workshopping

How often have you sat through CPD or a meeting and felt that the materials or content could be more interesting or engaging, or that you could do a better job running it yourself? You probably could! CPD is essentially what you do already on a daily basis as a teacher. You also likely do it with your colleagues, especially if you lead a subject, department, phase, or area.

Display work

Some of us are better at this than others. In some cases you may have been involved in set designs for school productions, but in all cases, you will have created your own display boards in your classroom or in communal areas. How creative are you with this? Translated into the outside world, this skill takes you to theatre design, window dressing, or curating. Yes, you will likely need to do some more training, but if you have a flair, you will have some great examples to share.

People skills

Not only are you creative with your people skills around your pupils, but you also manage hundreds of parents and an array of colleagues. You manage people, even if you think you don't. As a teacher you will likely manage learning-support assistants or other adults working in your classroom; as a year, phase, or subject lead, you will be managing and supporting the work of other teachers. You are actually very creative when it comes to people management, and this is a vital skill to take to a new workplace.

Training

You are great in front of not only young people, but also adults. Many of us have been directly involved in organising and running CPD and have also experienced those days on the receiving end, when we knew we could have run a better show. Teachers are often very creative trainers and organisers of CPD. The learning and development teams in more corporate contexts will bite your arm off for these kinds of skills.

Event management

Not only do you manage days and weeks of learning, but you'll also have organised trips and events, often on tight monetary and time budgets. Keeping pupils and/or adults fully engaged and entertained takes a huge amount of creative planning and management.

Specialist skills

During your time as a teacher, you will likely have developed many specialist skills to sit atop your transferrable skills and will know which aspects of your job you enjoy and which you don't. Why not take this as an opportunity to cherry-pick a focus and decide where your skills lie and what the options are, using these skills as a launch pad to a vast array of earning options.

Let's recap some of these options and the ways in which specialist skills developed within teaching roles can help forge a specialist path.

The Museum Education Officer

I always loved museums and spent a good chunk of my undergraduate degree studying primatology, evolution, social evolution, and material culture and artefacts. Straight out of my PGCE I was very fortunate to walk into an education role at a national museum, an opportunity which opened up a lot of doors and networks. I worked ad hoc for the education team while also teaching, until I took a permanent role as a member of the education team. On completing my MA in museum studies, I found it far easier to move up through the ranks.

Key skills/experiences:

- Teaching qualification
- Science background
- Understanding of artefacts and their interpretation
- Excellent communication skills
- MA in museum studies

The writer

I had experience, knowledge, and leadership skills in EYFS and KS1, with a broader understanding of KS2 as a subject lead. I also wanted to write. I loved planning lessons and creating resources – to a geeky extent. So I sought out opportunities to create outside of the classroom. My first offerings were pitched articles to well-respected education magazines, and after a couple were picked up and published, my journey began.

I then grabbed an opportunity to create planning materials for a support organisation and ultimately put all of these experiences together to present myself as a writer and ideas person, with a few years of in-school experience and curriculum knowledge.

Key skills/experiences:

- Qualified teacher
- Detailed knowledge of the education landscape
- Expertise in pedagogical themes and planning
- Subject-specific knowledge
- Excellent written skills
- High-level copy-editing skills
- Excellent communication skills
- Evidenced writing portfolio

The tutor

I loved the one-to-ones where I got to focus on pupils individually or in a group. I actually got really good at it. My skills developed and I started working as a tutor outside of school. The pressure was quite intense on top of my job, so I went part-time and switched to a mornings-only teaching role. This gave me the headspace to grow my tutoring business and have clear availability from 3pm. I would cover off three pupils an evening between 3pm and 7pm, four nights a week; then I did two pupils on a Saturday morning. Eventually, I set up a tutoring company for groups of children and employed more tutors.

Key skills/experience

- Qualified teacher
- Tutoring experience

- Strong pedagogical knowledge
- Subject specialism
- Experience of SATs, 11+, common entrance, GCSEs, and A-Levels

Out-of-school club leader

As an art teacher I loved my subject and wanted to continue to inspire and help children, so I started up an out-of-school club which ran mid-week evenings and Saturday afternoons. While it brought in an excellent hourly rate for me, I obviously wasn't raising a full-time salary. While there was a need to plan in advance and gather/purchase materials, I embedded this into the overall cost per child. I feel like I get the best of both worlds – none of the extras that come with teaching, but all of the satisfaction of guiding young artists to flourish and see them bloom.

Key skills/experience

- Qualified teacher
- Experience running children's clubs
- Strong pedagogical knowledge
- Subject specialism

Schools gardener/education officer

I ran eco-schools for years and the school gardening club, so it felt like a natural shift to work more in gardening. I completed some horticultural qualifications and shifted into a gardening apprenticeship. It was a drop in salary, but I also went on to run a local gardening club through the local authority as well as setting myself up as the freelance gardening club leader at my old school and two other local schools. Eventually I was employed by a local garden as an education officer.

Key skills/experience

- Qualified teacher
- Experience running children's garden clubs
- Experience running eco-schools or sustainability lead
- Strong pedagogical knowledge
- Subject specialism
- Gardening qualifications or knowledge

Outdoor education instructor

Training as a Forest School teacher meant that I got to spend a larger amount of my teaching time out in nature, inspiring young minds and championing sustainable lives. As an eco-schools leader as well, I eventually reduced my teaching role down to two days a week and run Forest School sessions on a freelance basis across other schools and nursery settings in the region. I often have the same groups of children in schools, so feel that I have a real rapport with many of the pupils.

Key skills/experience

- Qualified teacher
- Experience running outdoor sessions in school
- Experience running eco-schools or sustainability lead
- Strong pedagogical knowledge
- Subject specialism
- Forest School qualification

PE coach

As PE lead and a sports enthusiast outside of school, I used to be quite envious of the coaches that would come into school to run sessions, so decided that this was a good option for me. I took my coaching qualifications and now work part time for a coaching company, in local schools, and run my own after school, weekend and school holiday clubs. It is wonderful to see children progressing and developing as sports people and enables me to focus on my pure passion

Key skills/experience

- Qualified teacher
- PE lead
- Experience running sports clubs in school
- Strong pedagogical knowledge
- Subject specialism
- Coaching qualifications

Theatre workshop lead

I was head of drama in a large secondary and spent much of my own time involved in local drama groups and productions. I directed and produced multiple successful shows a year at my school for over ten years before applying for a freelance position at a national theatre to run workshops for schools, reducing my in-school commitments right down. After a year or so, I launched my own drama school and run weekly drama for primary and secondary age children.

Key skills/experience

- Qualified teacher
- Drama lead
- Out-of-school theatrical experience
- Strong pedagogical knowledge
- Subject specialism
- Exceptional communication skills

Training and CPD

Running in-school CPD was always a strength of mine – I loved organising workshops and inspiring my colleagues. Inspired by my head suggesting I take some LA training sessions, I began doing more and more outside of my own school. I now run my own training company, with contracts in local schools; I run some of the sessions myself and bring in others to run sessions as well.

Key skills/experience

- Qualified and experienced teacher
- Detailed knowledge of the education landscape
- Strong pedagogical knowledge
- Subject or area specialisms
- Experience developing and running in-school CPD
- Exceptional communication skills

Lecturer

I spent seven years in an early-years classroom before applying to a local higher education college to train learning support assistants (LSAs). I had spent a good number of years line managing and delivering in-house mentoring and training to LSAs and ECTs.

After a successful career in schools as a teacher and headteacher, I was particularly interested in supporting ECTs and trainee teachers. I had worked closely with local initial teacher training settings and colleges, working as a visiting lecturer. Once I reached a point where I felt I needed a change in direction, I took on a role as a university tutor and began undertaking research which led to my current role as a full lecturer in education.

Key skills/experience

- Qualified and experienced teacher
- Detailed knowledge of the education landscape
- Strong pedagogical knowledge
- Subject or area specialisms
- Experience mentoring students and early career teachers (ECTs)
- Exceptional communication skills

How to find your freelance "thing"

Working out not only what you'd like to do but also what you have the skills for takes careful consideration. You need to take a good, long, hard look at yourself, what you like, what you dislike, where you know you have skills, and where you have potential. It is also important to reflect honestly on where you don't have skills and whether this is an area you'd like to shift away from or to bolster up. I would recommend creating a "wish board" over a period of time – a month, say – as this will help give a far more detailed and honest assessment. Use the following questions to inform the wish board, and stick it on the fridge or somewhere prominent so that you can reflect on it daily. This is a soul-searching exercise that will help you identify strengths, weaknesses, and areas where you thrive and where you don't. Combine this with your SOAP analysis from Chapter One and you will be well on your way to identifying your "thing".

- I am interested in …
- I've always wanted to …

- I am good at ...
- I have skills in ...
- I am experienced in ...
- I would like more experience in ...

Forging your path

Once you have identified your niche knowledge and your transferrable and specialist skills, consider what you could do to make them and you stand out. Could you complete a course or offer to hone some of these skills in your current role? Always look for opportunities to hero these skills; such opportunities will have an immediate impact in your current job and also help you along the way.

If you decide to begin a freelance journey, keep track of which skills you already have and enjoy and which ones you'd like to develop. I still find I am forging a path, discovering the things I love doing and specialist training I may wish to undertake. And, in fact, some things shift as we move forward. When you do something for a long period of time, even though you once enjoyed it, it may become repetitive and boring, or you may just fall out of love with it. That's ok, and actually it is something that keeps us going.

I like to have a visual-skills chart to keep me thinking and forging forwards. Figure 4.1 sets out the things I enjoy and dislike as well as those solid skills I already possess and those that still need work.

Heroing your skills

Once you have identified your skills and started to forge a path, it may yet take time for these to become fully formed in a new career or earning opportunity. Over the years I have heroed specific skills that have evolved and developed into new and exciting opportunities along the way. I have shared these here to give you a flavour of how skills development can evolve and forge your path.

	AMAZING SKILLS	*SKILLS NEED DEVELOPING*
ENJOY	Writing	Copy editing
	Research	Script writing
	Working with people	
DISLIKE	Proofing	Workshopping
	Presenting	Strategy
	Running CPD	

Figure 4.1 Skills chart for Fe Luton

Planning and writing

I used to love planning – I was quite obsessed. I loved coming up with creative ideas and creating exciting and fun ways to approach teaching, especially in those areas where sometimes the learning could feel a little dry. Back when I was in the classroom, commercial schemes of work were not really a thing. We worked from the National Literacy Strategy and the Numeracy Strategy, but beyond using workbooks and a teachers book for maths, we were fully free-range. I spent hours devising long- and medium-term plans and took immense pleasure weaving in the progression while making the learning real and exciting for children (and for me).

This passion and experience led to:

- Writing up ideas for education magazines
- Writing English plans for a corporate organisation

This experience led to:

- Becoming a paid education researcher and writer

This experience led to:

- Going freelance and writing articles, resources, lessons, and schemes of work for a range of organisations. Includes writing two books full of ideas for school clubs

This experience led to:

- A role as a senior content writer, developing and creating resources and programmes for schools

Research and the education landscape

I have always been fascinated by education research, and when I took on my first subject lead role, I did *a lot* of research. I fed off of what was out there and devoured new policies, ideas, pedagogies, and resources. All of this helped me to create effective schemes of work and find exciting resources to help run the best lessons we could. When faced with problems to solve, research was my go-to.

This passion and experience led to:

- Becoming a paid education researcher and writer

This experience led to:

- Going freelance and writing articles, resources, lessons, and schemes of work for a range of organisations

This experience led to:

- Director of Research and Content at Subject Leaders and education landscape specialist, undertaking research to share insights

Project management

I have always loved organising things. During my time as a museum education officer, it was workshops, exhibition launches, and resources, while as a teacher it was trips, schemes of work, training days, and social events for staff. As a researcher and writer, I demonstrated this skill in web projects, writing books, creating courses, and the like.

This passion and experience led to:

- Managing a wide range of freelance projects

This experience led to:

- Setting up my own business developing web content

It is key that you find your passion to ensure that whatever moves you make are made for the right reasons - pulls not pushes. By identifying your niche knowledge and specialist skills, you are setting a path that will continue to develop you professionally.

5 So you want to go freelance ...

Jumping on the freelance train

With the hybrid working world we now live in, 'going freelance' feels less of a jump than it perhaps once was. In fact, from the outside, many employed jobs appear quite freelance these days, with flexible working hours and so many work-from-home options.

What exactly do we mean by freelance, though? The classic version of being freelance is having work channelled through a range of organisations or businesses, usually in the form of commissions or projects. However, being freelance can take on a range of structures, and for the purposes of this book, we are going as broad as we can. Options might include:

- Full-time freelance (multiple projects for multiple "clients")
- Part-time employment and part-time freelance
- Full-time employment with freelance projects on the side (the 'side hustle')
- Rolling freelance contracts (the "perma-lance" option)
- Zero-hour contracts (for example, being "employed" by the local authority as a supply teacher)
- Contracted for a set number of freelance workshop sessions a month or term
- Running your own business (technically self-employed, but to all intents and purposes, you are freelance)

Why go freelance?

There are plenty of positives to working in some kind of freelance capacity:

- Being your own boss
- Working the hours you choose
- Selecting work that interests you
- Earning a decent daily rate
- Generally getting paid for the hours you put in
- Injecting variety into your work
- Taking days off when you fancy them
- Having the flexibility to own your work
- The opportunity to work wherever you like

DOI: 10.4324/9781003378334-5

But it is also not something to shift into without careful consideration. It's important that you understand your reasons for becoming freelance and stick by this rationale. Think to yourself, is it a pull or a push? I went fully freelance partly because of my personal circumstances. I had the flexibility to work random hours across the day, as long as I could be available at a moment's notice. There had always been a pull towards freelance work, but up until that point, job security had been a stronger pull.

I also knew I had the back up of supply teaching, which many other professions don't have – an option that gives you some security but enough wriggle room to say no if you need to. This was a lifeline and not an option to be sneezed at.

If you are thinking seriously about a shift, whether it is a small shift or a greater leap, I would highly recommend carry out a SWOT (Strengths, Weaknesses, Opportunities, Threats) analysis of your current role vs a freelance role to sit alongside the SOAP analysis we did in Chapter One. Your SOAP analysis identifies what you could do, while your SWOT analysis helps you to understand the reality of shifting to a freelance career. Figure 5.1 sets out the SWOT analysis I completed in 2013, when I went full-time freelance.

There is no doubt that you will need resolve and determination to build a freelance portfolio, but once you start to establish yourself in the freelance education world, the fight for work becomes easier.

STRENGTHS	WEAKNESSES
• I already have some contacts and two streams of "side hustle" income • I have experience of education writing and training outside of school • I have a good level of in-school education experience that would be appealing to potential clients • Personal circumstances are pushing me to make this work	• My writing skills need further development • Networking up to this point hasn't come easily to me • I'm not very good at marketing myself

OPPORTUNITIES	THREATS
• Existing freelance streams could grow • I have lots of contacts who I could approach to run training • Focusing on freelance work would help build my skills	• I could end up with an irregular or low income • I could struggle to find work • I can't work set times

Figure 5.1 SWOT analysis for Fe Luton, 2013

What to do?

This is the moment to look back through the options outlined in Chapter Two and to reflect on the skills, experiences, interests, and niche knowledge, identified in Chapter Four, that you'd like to monopolise on. The sky's the limit when it comes to freelance: you may decide that you want to dabble in more than one thing or that you want to specialise in something specific and work on a range of projects within that.

Deciding on your freelance working week

When you go freelance one of the biggest shifts is that you own your working week. You decide how much work you want, when you want to do it, and, to a degree, what you want to do. This will all be dependent on the type of freelancer you are. Up until relatively recently, I was in the full-time category of freelancer but also ran my own business. A typical day for me usually included:

- 4:00–6:30 freelance writing (2.5 hours)
- 6:30–8:30 child management and my household jobs for the day
- 08:30–09:00 walk (often with a friend)
- 09:00–15:30 freelance writing (lunch at my desk) (6.5 hours)
- 15:30 onwards children, clubs, household jobs, me time

You can see from this that my working day was around nine hours. I found it quite easy to work a nine-hour day, and it meant that, in theory, I could have a half-day somewhere across the week when I didn't need to work. This worked for me, and after the heavy structure and commitment of a teaching career, a complete change felt refreshing. For others the day would look different, perhaps with evening work, or even weekend work, if that suits your commitments better.

I then shifted into rolling freelance work (the perma-lancer) which led to a part-time employed hybrid role, alongside part-time freelance work and running my business. My working day looks different as a result and I tend to go swimming or walking in the lunch hour that I now take, meaning my workday finishes a bit later.

All versions have their pros and cons, and for me, being fully freelance while my children were very young was the perfect fit. Now that my children are older, having a hybrid employed role alongside freelance work is more manageable (and enjoyable). It's about finding what works best for you.

Being successful

To succeed as a freelancer, the writer Neil Gaiman[1] suggests that you need to aim for at least two of three key things if you want to be successful:

- Be easy to work with
- Produce work of a high standard
- Always meet deadlines

> "You get work however you get work, but people keep working in a free-lance world, ... because their work is good, because they are easy to get along with and because they deliver the work on time. And you don't even need all three! Two out of three is fine."

He goes on to eloquently explain the reality of this:

> "People will tolerate how unpleasant you are if your work is good and you deliver it on time. People will forgive the lateness of your work if it is good and they like you. And you don't have to be as good as everyone else if you're on time and it's always a pleasure to hear from you."

He suggests that if you can hit two of these things, you should succeed and continue to get work. Obviously if you are utterly hideous to work with the other two might not be enough, just as always missing deadlines by a long way, or producing work of a spectacularly appalling standard, is unlikely to send clients rushing to rebook your services! But I always keep these three things in mind with every client and piece of work I produce. As a mantra I have always adopted, it has so far served me well.

What are the downsides to going freelance?

While working as a freelancer conjures up an idyllic lifestyle, the reality can be slightly more sobering:

- Say goodbye to sick pay, pensions, and holiday pay
- Say goodbye (often) to colleagues
- Say goodbye to your workspace
- Say goodbye to work and income security
- Say goodbye to external motivation
- Work boundaries disappear
- Overwork can become a real issue
- Career progression can stall
- CPD is no longer on offer unless you pay for it yourself

Let's have a look at these in more detail.

Say goodbye to sick pay, pensions, and holiday pay

Sick pay, pension payments, and holiday pay are no longer someone else's concern when you go freelance. It all needs to come from what you earn, and in order to make it work, you need to plan carefully for all these eventualities.

Let's do the maths

A £40,000 teaching role actually costs your school £45,000+ to cover these "extra" costs. That's over 10% of your pay. So, when you set a freelance day rate, you not only need to consider the tax and National Insurance that you will owe but you need to consider any other "contingency" you will need.

Let's look at it like this:

A £40,000 salary is just under £155 a day before tax (assuming you received that every working/holiday day of the year).

That seems feasible. But let's now do the calculation with five weeks holiday and five days sick a year – that's 30 less days of pay.

To earn our £40,000 salary, we now need to earn just under £175 a day before tax and National Insurance.

Next up is a pension contribution – say 10% (because, remember, you have no employer contribution).

To earn our £40,000 salary, we now need to earn £189 a day.

But with this day rate, we are assuming that you always have work. I'd recommend adding in a contingency for that as well to cover any downtime you have. Say 10%.

So, after all that, we've smashed through £200 for a day rate to create an equivalent freelance salary of £40,000.

Possible solutions

It is crucial not only that you factor these costs in, but that when you earn money, you also siphon it off and ensure it either goes into a rainy-day (holidays and sick pay) bank account or is fed directly into a pension scheme.

Say goodbye to colleagues

This is actually the hardest part of freelance work and one I have struggled with in the past. The appeal of working your own hours and at home may sound like you're living the dream, but actually the reality can be far from it.

Without colleagues to draw you in and to a degree "hold you to account", you'll suddenly find a thousand and one distractions around the house, and in a multi-person living set-up, be it a partner, family with children, or flatmates, the fact that you are working from home, and freelance, may mean that certain daily tasks seem to fall at your door. The expectation that you can drop everything because you are not directly employed can play in your favour at times, but it can also play against you.

I discovered that colleagues are also good at helping you set boundaries – they remind you to go home; they listen to your woes about workload and help you gain perspective; they remind you to take a break. Freelance work holds no boundaries and without the wisdom of colleagues around you to help, you may find it hard to create those boundaries for yourself.

It's also very easy to lose focus without company. Sometimes solitude is nice (my partner works from home two days a week, so actually I quite enjoy the peace and quiet the other days), but at times it is important from a productivity perspective to talk to others and take a brain break from what you are doing. Talking about the mundane and day-to-day is what you will miss the most about colleagues. It can be very isolating when you do some work but can't chat to someone about it and run ideas past them.

Freelance work can get very boring if you are working on the same kinds of project over and over again. Writing and teacher-resource development – my initial foray – could be really exciting at times but mind-numbingly boring at others. You may find yourself looking back nostalgically on those staff meetings that drove you nuts and the quick cuppa in the staffroom between lessons. Losing your colleagues not only impacts levels of loneliness but can also impact your boredom, simply because you have no-one to talk to or have a good moan with.

Possible solutions

- Buddying up online with others who work freelance, through buddying schemes or local freelancers' networks, can really help
- Work outside the home in a social space (cafés, libraries)
- Go to a shared workspace, or rent a desk at a local business
- Get freelance work with a client who is happy for you to pop into the office now and again
- Arrange to meet friends for lunch or coffee breaks
- Get yourself a workspace buddy – someone who you could take turns working from one another's homes or heading to a workspace together

Say goodbye to your workspace

The ideal workspaces for a freelancer might include: a pod at the bottom of the garden; a dedicated office away from your living space; or a hot desk that you can hire. In reality you will likely be sitting at the kitchen table, so you need to find ways to create work boundaries that are attainable and sustainable. I sometimes work in a café (if I have no meetings and the price of food and drink across the hours doesn't bankrupt me, and always bringing headphones just in case,). I have a couple of regular haunts where the staff openly welcome me in and go out of their way to make me feel at home. This not only creates a personal workspace boundary but also gives you a set of people with whom you build a relationship during your working day. Pseudo-colleagues, if you like! I tend to do this once a week to get out of the house.

Possible solutions

- Working outside of the home – the library, cafés, dedicated desk for hire spaces
- Create a specific space within your home that is dedicated to work and separate from your personal and family spaces
- Clear work away into a cupboard at the end of your working day so that it is no longer visible in your home space

Say goodbye to work and income security

Work and income security disappears as a freelancer, and this will, without doubt, feel very unnerving and stressful to start with. It takes some getting used to, but once you get into the swing of things and you build relationships with clients so that regular work becomes more common than not, you will find the panic subsides. Having multiple streams of income is key, unless you can find a rolling or semi-agile contract. Over the years, I have found a range of effective routes that ease the stress of irregular commissions.

Possible solutions

- Ask for work before you have a gap – clients will usually take longer than a day to respond and may need to prepare a brief in advance
- Block out your days as far in advance as you can
- Don't be afraid to have conversations about work stream/flow from clients, once you have built your relationship
- Taking on long-deadline projects can really help fill sudden gaps
- Put out feelers to other potential clients if you can see a gap coming up
- Try not to panic, and always have a supply-teaching back-up plan

Say goodbye to external motivation

You need to turn yourself into a super-human self-motivator if you want to work freelance. When you are not expected to be through the office/classroom door by a certain time, it makes life harder to structure. And when you have no-one to hold you to account, it is very easy to develop high-level procrastination skills. Self-motivation is a hard one, especially when you are isolated or you hit a spell of boredom, meaning it is important to adopt some strategies to ensure you are held to account.

Laying out your day and setting clears goals can help, as can chunking up your work into 45-minute slots. If you can't face a whole day on one thing, this is where being freelance on multiple projects can come into its own - mix up what work you are doing, when. As long as you meet your deadlines, you have the privilege of deciding when you do your work.

Possible solutions

- Set yourself a start time and always have your day planned
- Get outside at some point during the day and have a time that you "leave the office"
- Create a checklist of what you want/need to achieve for the day
- Always complete the tasks you least like in the morning
- Find a way to organise your week that helps motivate you

Work boundaries can be tricky

Working from home can create huge problems with home/work boundaries. I learnt this the hard way and found myself permanently "on". As the world has shifted more towards a hybrid way of working, we find more and more of us are setting up our workspace in the home, and, actually, for those of us who have been doing this for years, there is a sense of security in numbers and that working boundaries at home are becoming better understood and respected.

Try to be self-aware of boundaries and find a multitude of ways to define them - this can be anything from setting strict work hours to "putting work away" at the end of a day.

Possible solutions

- Working outside of the home - the library, cafés, dedicated desk-for-hire spaces
- Setting yourself boundaries, be it working hours or maximum weekly workloads
- Setting highly defined hours for work - set an alarm to tell you the day is over
- Having somewhere to store your work so that it isn't visible when you are on "home" hours

Overwork can become a real issue

Saying no to work is not impossible but can be very tricky, especially early on in your freelance career when you are building up your workflow. I didn't say no for a very long time and sometimes half-killed myself to meet deadlines and massive workloads. There are a few ways to avoid overwork, though:

- Try to negotiate longer deadlines - clients are usually open to this unless it is a tight turnaround
- Always try to set deadlines for a Monday morning, not a Friday afternoon. That way, in an emergency, you still have the weekend
- Do say "not now" - explain that your work calendar is rammed this week but that you could do it at a later point, or that if there is other work they need doing, you could do that at a later point
- Renegotiate with other deadlines - clients who don't have tight turnarounds are often very open to you asking for extensions that then allow you to re-prioritise other work

Career progression can stall

When you are running your own ship, it is easy to lose track of your direction and skills development. All of your new work will push you forwards to begin with, but you need to think carefully about where you see yourself in five or ten years and what you need to be doing to get there. We explored this in Chapter Three, highlighting that the key is planning out a career path.

Possible solutions

- Create a career path
- Map out skills development
- Give yourself annual reviews

CPD is no longer on offer unless you pay for it yourself

Linked into your career development is CPD. This will automatically disappear off your radar if you are used to your school paying for it or having easy access to it. CPD continues to be important, and much though it may pain you to pay for it yourself, it is an important part of developing as a freelancer.

Possible solutions

- Create a CPD money pot, and pay into it every month
- Keep an eye out for courses you'd like to attend (online tends to be cheaper)
- Look for free or cheap CPD options - many education shows, like the BETT show, are free to attend and have lots of talks. Alternatively, organisations such as FutureLearn offer plenty of free training options

- Ex-heads you have worked for may be happy for you to join in their CPD, if it is of relevance to you, for a reduced cost; or, better still, you can offer to run some CPD in exchange for attending CPD

Weighing up the pros and the cons

While that may feel like a big, long list of cons for freelance work, the pros are definitely very strong, and, in fact, as we have seen, there are solutions to all the cons. If you are not sure that you want to fully risk a complete dive into freelance life, why not dip your toe in the water with a freelance side hustle? In the next chapter we explore ways to manage this while remaining in the classroom.

Note

1   Neil Gaiman: Keynote Address 2012 | University of the Arts (uarts.edu).

6 So you want a side hustle ...

Becoming a freelancer may sound appealing, but what if you're not sure you're ready (or financially prepared) for the plunge?

The side hustle option

It is a huge leap to shift from a fully paid, employed teaching role to a fully freelance adventure, which is why "side hustle" freelance work has a great appeal as a middle-ground option to many teachers, allowing them to:

- Earn some extra cash
- Develop some new skills
- Dabble in a new field
- Top up a part-time teaching role
- Test the waters for a long-term escape plan

Not only is it a great way to dip your toe in the water, but it can actually be really fun. I started out doing bits and pieces alongside my full-time teaching job, creating lesson plans for organisations and writing articles for education publications, before gradually shifting towards a greater proportion of freelance work and ultimately a full-time freelance world:

- Full-time teacher with some ad hoc freelance resource development and article writing on the side
- Full-time employed education writer
- Part-time teacher, part-time freelance writer
- Full-time freelance writer
- Employed writer, business owner, freelance writer

When I began doing additional freelance "side hustle" work, I had no family commitments and could dedicate time at the weekend to complete projects and commissions. It's a big commitment if you have jam-packed weekends and evenings, and it does demand dedicated time, which can add to the pressure already experienced by teachers.

If you are anticipating a shift towards the freelance world while holding onto your classroom reins, remember to take your time and not jump at the first thing that comes along, and be careful not to take on an immense additional workload.

DOI: 10.4324/9781003378334-6

Side hustle practicalities

Before embarking on a "side hustle" journey, there are a few things you'll need to give careful consideration to. If you are doing freelance work while employed at a school, you'll need to reflect on:

- Informing your employer
- Mentioning your school
- Copyright and use of school property (intellectual and physical)
- Tax commitments

Do I have to tell my employer?

You'll need to check your contract. Generally speaking you don't need to declare anything unless there is a conflict of interest (for example, tutoring one of the children in your class or working for a parent may create a conflict of interest). It is always best practise to declare up front any extra work you do that may connect to school; that way, everyone is in the loop.

Of course most schools and headteachers will be delighted for you to discuss options with them, and, actually, if it raises the profile of the school, they may be happy for you to adapt certain things and share them as best practise or be the education authority on something. For example, if you are a subject lead and, quite frankly, you are really good at it, know your stuff, and have been supporting others both in and out of school, there is no reason why you can't use this expertise to draft articles or run CPD. But if the school is taking on a supporting role in this, they may expect some benefits.

Can I mention my school and current role in articles etc?

I would always clear this with your headteacher. Some love the good publicity while others will be more wary. You can always create a by-line that gives your role and region or call yourself something new entirely – education specialist or education writer.

What are the rules around copyright and use of school property?

You need to consider carefully what you are doing, who you are doing it for, and what you are using to do it. Sounds cryptic, but don't slip into a tricky situation where your employer (local authority, academy, or trust) could potentially discipline you for breach of copyright or use of work resources. I realise that sounds quite dramatic, but if you check your contract, you will likely find there are rules around stuff you have created for your current classroom and using school equipment (yes, that includes tech) that technically belongs to your school, MAT, or LA. Essentially, they own the copyright.

There are certain things you simply can't do and could get yourself into hot water for trying:

- Lifting your planning from school and selling it - the school pays you to create the planning so technically they own it; it is their intellectual property
- Using a school laptop to create your own resources/articles - it is their equipment and mustn't be used for your own work
- Selling a resource you made to teach in a lesson - again, the school pays you to do that so has a right to "own" it

That's not to say that you couldn't take an idea or something you have created and redraft it for resale on your own time and your own computer. Many schools are very open to celebrating success through article writing, CPD, or sharing resources, especially when it raises the profile of the school.

For things directly from your school (planning etc) you may be able to get the school "paid" in books, for example. I did this a few times when I wrote articles, as I was building my portfolio and raising my profile. My headteacher loved it, as did the library!

Will I need to pay tax on any additional income?

Technically if you earn £1000 or more in additional income not connected to your salary, HMRC will want to know about it[1], and you'll have to fill in a self-assessment tax return. No matter what you earn, it is always worth calling HMRC just to double check - they are, despite the rumours, really helpful and will give you peace of mind. Filling out a self-assessment tax return is not as scary as it sounds to the uninitiated, and actually just requires a bit of organisation and a couple of hours to get your paperwork together. Don't take up an opportunity because of the tax implications or paperwork - it really isn't that much of a chore.

What works well as a side hustle and how to break into it ...

Whatever your niche knowledge and specialist skills are, remember that a side hustle needs to be something you can fit into your working week. Some common options include:

- Writing articles
- Writing resources
- Tutoring
- Researching

- Marking exams
- Sports coaching
- Consultancy
- CPD
- Museum/gallery workshop teacher
- Outdoor education
- Out-of-school clubs
- Higher education
- Proof reading
- Teacher panels and reviewing

Writing articles

You're going to need some ideas and you're going to need to write well. It is a competitive area, but good, creative, and unique ideas can go a long way. Treat it like any other job and allow yourself time to reflect on areas you would like to and can write about and areas that you know teachers or senior leaders want to hear about. Write textbooks, write phonics scheme books, write a novel, write articles, write plans.

Resource development

There are two versions of this: creating resources for established curriculum companies or creating resources for organisations or publishing houses that offer miscellaneous teaching resources. You can also go it alone, creating your own resources and marketing them yourself or via a site such as the TES.

Tutoring

Always check in with the rules your headteacher, trust, or local authority have set around this. Find clients via word of mouth or approach a tutoring agency.

Researcher

Teachers make great researchers, when it comes to the education landscape or areas in and around pedagogy. The small-piece opportunities are not abundant but definitely worth looking for if you have particularly strong research skills.

Marking exams

This can work whichever phase you teach in. SATs, Common Entrance, 11+, 13+, GCSEs and A-levels all need professionals to mark them. While it can be a lot of work at the time, it can bring in some extra cash and isn't a year-round commitment.

Writing assessment papers

Many organisations that set papers employ teachers to help write them, from formal examination papers to buy-into assessment packages. You'll need to be fairly experienced for this one, but it is a great option for piece-meal work.

Sports coaching

While not always paid at the level of a teacher, sports coaching is a great option if you have time before or after school or at the weekends to fit it in; team sports, swimming, gymnastics, or dance are all great options, if you have the right qualifications.

Consultant

If you have experience in a management position or have a specialism that other schools could benefit from – tech, creative curriculum development, or safeguarding, for example – especially within a successful school, you will be in a position to set yourself up as a consultant for local authorities, trusts, MATs, or individual schools. This could take the form of one-off consultancies or an ongoing relationship.

CPD

Running CPD for other schools through your school is an option, but it tends to be paid directly into your salary, and the school takes a cut. You could alternatively go it alone and offer CPD days, twilight sessions, or online courses for teachers. You may also find that local authorities or regional providers may be keen to take you on to run courses in their subscribed schools.

Museum/gallery workshop teacher

Many museums or galleries employ freelance education facilitators. They really like these to be teachers or ex-teachers and to have age-specific or subject-specific expertise. Look out for freelance opportunities on museum or gallery websites or contact them directly yourself to enquire – they'll usually have a pool of freelancers. Roles will likely be during school hours, but some family workshops may run at the weekends.

Outdoor education

Forest school or outdoor centre teachers are often freelancers in the same way that museum or gallery workshop facilitators are. Contact local organisations directly to see if they have any openings in out-of-school hours.

Before- and after-school clubs

Plenty of schools are happy to bring in pay-for clubs to offer for parents. These can prove especially popular with parents if you are offering extra opportunities for skills or experiences beyond those the school curriculum covers – for example, art, drama, sports, gardening, and languages. But make sure you have a solid background in the area, as this will not only make your life easier but also add to your status as club organiser. Additionally, look at the options of running clubs in community centres. Be careful of things like insurance, though, and be prepared for classroom-style behaviour management. You also need to consider the time for prep, any resources you need to pay for, and whether you'll run sessions in the holidays.

Higher education

Universities often employ visiting lecturers or freelance education Initial Teacher Training (ITT) tutors for those with substantial classroom experience, in-school ITT tutoring or mentoring, and middle/senior management.

Proofreading

If you are an English teacher, or particularly good with your SPaG skills, then proofreading may be a great option. There are lots of freelance projects and agencies that would keep the workflow going.

Teacher panels and reviewing

Plenty of organisations need teachers to review what they create, or to give opinions and ideas from a teacher's perspective. This can prove quite lucrative, and often only requires an hour or so of your time. Agencies often organise this kind of work, and it is satisfying to get your expert opinion across.

How to manage a side-hustle (when you're teaching full time)

As teachers, we already have a hefty workload. It isn't exactly a nine-to-five that starts and ends with a resounding clunk. Being a teacher is hard work, and finding extra hours in the week if you are still full-time requires careful planning. When working full time in the classroom:

- Find a dedicated time that you are happy to earmark or rope off. Plan it in and stick to it
- Organise your school working week so that you are running as efficiently as possible
- Look carefully at your working week and consider non-negotiable commitments that you'll need to work around – if you have parent consultations, for example, you might want to make sure you haven't committed to other work that week. Or when it is report season, you are going to need all your time for school writing
- Ring-fence how much time you will spend on extra pieces of "side hustle" work – if you plan it to take two hours, make sure it doesn't take longer than two hours

How to manage a side-hustle (when you're teaching part time)

The game changes slightly when you work part-time and want to top up with freelance work. And, really, it is up to you how you want to play it. There are plenty of approaches:

- Carefully earmark the work-week hours you are not in the classroom to complete your freelance work
- Keep your non-teaching hours as days off and fit your freelance work in at the weekend or evenings
- Some kind of hybrid of the two above

You do still need to consider flashpoints in the school year, though, when your work hours seep into your days off because of report writing, planning, subject leadership, and the like. Work shouldn't intrude on your time off, but, with the best will in the world, we all know that it does.

In the next chapter we explore in greater detail the practicalities of freelance work.

Note

1   Everyone has a tax-free trading allowance of £1000, meaning anything you earn up to £1000 in a side hustle is not taxable. Anything over £1000 will require a self-assessment for HMRC.

7 The practicalities of freelance work

Your freelance dream may be alive and well, but the reality still needs some thought. In this chapter it's time for housekeeping: all those things that need to go on behind the scenes to make any freelance journey work in the real world. In this chapter we look at some of the practicalities and considerations you'll need to think about and the realities of some of the options available. Let's start with money.

Money

Money is always going to be at the heart of any work-related conversation, and in the freelance world more so than anywhere else. From earning an equivalent teaching salary to billing rates, tax, and other hidden costs, there is plenty to talk about, when it comes to money.

Earning an equivalent salary or taking a hit

If you are changing jobs entirely, you are going to want a salary equivalent to your teaching salary. Or, if you can afford to take a drop, you need to bear in mind the opportunity gains of the shift; this is important to ensure you don't start to resent any new job that pays less and wish you had never made the change. I took a pay cut on two occasions when leaving the classroom, but I rationalised it by calculating an hourly rate for the actual number of hours I worked in teaching to the actual number of hours I would work in my new role (this included the holidays and a realistic reflection on the number of hours I worked in school in the holidays, as well).

Here's how it went down:

> **Teacher hours/week** (with holiday adjustments – average of one to two days' work per week of holiday): 47 hours/week spread over 52 weeks.
> **Teacher salary** (through threshold and with TLRs): £40,000.
> £40,000 ÷ 52 ÷ 47 = **£16/hr**
>
> **Researcher/writer hours/week** (with holiday adjustment – no work during holidays): 33 hours/week over 52 weeks.
> **Researcher/writer salary:** £33,000
> £33,000 ÷ 52 ÷ 33 = **£19/hr**

DOI: 10.4324/9781003378334-7

It's interesting doing this exercise, as you may decide, if you have gone from time-poor to time-rich, to take on a different role and then top up in other ways.

But if the reality is that you need the same salary regardless of the hours, you will need to think carefully about your next move. Some "ex-teacher" roles are very poorly paid and do not acknowledge the skills and expertise you have, while demanding those skills nonetheless. Other employers recognise the value (both in monetary terms and in terms of kudos within their organisation) of ex-teachers and offer salaries more on a par with the teacher pay-scale. Don't be afraid to ask for an equivalent salary if it is within the range on offer, but do be cognisant of the fact that many ranges will start towards the bottom. With that said, it is also worth considering what the scope to progress is, as you may find that, actually, your salary will grow and catch up with your teaching equivalent within a relatively short period of time.

How much am I worth? – freelance rates

If you are taking the freelance route – either some work on the side, or a full shift – make sure you take time to carefully consider your rates. As we explored in Chapter Five, there are lots of hidden costs with freelance, especially if it becomes your main source of income, and you will need to land on a rate that works for you financially but also reflects your experience. It is hard to put yourself out there and say what you are worth without apologising or caving at the first challenge or hurdle. You'll also need to consider that different levels of expertise and different tasks or types of work will require different rates. Figure 7.1 shows the relative rates of a range of freelance roles.

Working out your billing rate can feel stressful. A good starting point is what you would get as a daily rate if you were supply teaching. When I started out, I calculated my worth based on what I would earn doing supply teaching for a day *in the private sector*. This is generally higher than state school rates and now that you are essentially shifting into the private or corporate sector, you need to

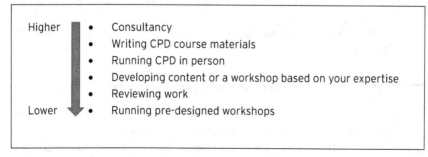

Figure 7.1 Relative billable rates by role

be a bit bolder in what you ask for. Also, don't forget to add onto this for extras such as sick pay, holiday pay, and down times. From this baseline, make sure you have a figure in mind for a range of billable options:

- **Per hour** - this will tend to be higher than a day rate, simply because it is not a guarantee of a day's work. It also may differ from job to job and from organisation to organisation
- **Per day** - this will be close to your hourly rate ÷ 7.5 but I usually round down, simply because it is a guaranteed day of work. So, if I was charging £35/hour, I might charge a day at £260 - it's just a couple of pounds under my hourly rate, but employers will appreciate the gesture (plus your day may end up being eight to nine hours, and your day rate won't change as a result)
- **Per project** - this is the hardest one to work out. Sometimes it is dictated to you (in which case do some careful calculating before you agree, and definitely haggle where possible), but other times you may be asked to quote for a job. It is *very* easy to underestimate this one, and unless it is a project with a set number of hours, it is worth taking the time to calculate how long you think the project will take ... then add on 50% of that. It is human nature to hugely underestimate, and I can guarantee that you will. Trust me: I learnt the hard way on a project that ended up being a £7/hour job by the time I had finished it. I became very frustrated and angry with that project, but also learnt a valuable lesson.

I also found myself having slightly different approaches to different types of organisations, as well. Charities don't have as much disposable income, so I tend to bill lower for them - I don't have to, but I choose to. Corporate organisations have much greater pools of money to spend on freelancers, so this is where I bill my full worth. I will also accept a lower rate if:

1. The work is amazingly fun and I really want to do it
2. I know the work is more long-term, and I have an almost guaranteed income (it is worth seeking out rolling "perma-lance" contracts in this situation)
3. I know the work will expose me massively and likely get me more (and better paid) work elsewhere

Remember your hourly rate as you work

When you start working freelance, you understandably want to make a good impression by creating something amazing. It is important, though, that you keep to your timings, otherwise your earnings start to become negligible, and you *will* get frustrated. Sometimes you'll be over time and others under - it will all even itself out so long as you are strict with yourself and plan your time carefully. If you need to complete it in four hours to make it financially viable, then it really needs to be in or around that ballpark. I usually break this down into research, plan, draft, final draft, final edits. It will also help you to understand how long things take to do and where you may need to negotiate different rates.

What is my take home?

When you start freelancing and billing you may initially feel like you are "in the money", as all of the money is coming to you. Under no circumstances get into the mindset that you have actually just earned that amount of money. You haven't! You need to consider:

- Tax and National Insurance
- Sick pay
- Holiday pay
- Barren periods of time (down time)
- Pensions
- Non-billable time
- Pay rises

I've set out in what follows the main considerations for each of these, but individual circumstances will need consideration.

Tax and National Insurance

The chances are that, up until now, you won't have had to think much about tax and National Insurance, as it comes out of your pay before the money hits your bank. If you are earning a freelance salary or even a bit on the side, you'll need to make friends with HMRC. Despite the agency's reputation, I have never found completing a tax return burdensome.

What do I need to pay tax on? Everything you have earned above the tax allowance threshold.

How is National Insurance calculated? You'll be asked about this when you fill out your tax return and will be billed accordingly.

What records will I need to keep? Having clear records of your earnings (I keep this in the form of my invoices) is the key to an easy tax return. You'll need to keep receipts as well, and, if you are working from home, you can also factor in a proportion of your energy bills.

Do I need an accountant? No. Once you have had a look online at HMRC and filed your first tax return, you'll find managing it yourself is generally the most practical approach.

When should I do my tax return? Not in January! I have done this a few times, and it can be stressful as your tax needs to be paid by the 31st of January. You may need to reset passwords or you have underestimated how much you owe, so doing it well in advance of this deadline gives you greater wriggle toom. I try to do my in May-June, which gives me six months to come up with the cash if I am short.

I have heard that HMRC want money up front. I'm afraid this one is true. Be prepared for a shock on your first tax bill, as they will want the next six months' worth of tax at that point; but then it evens out.

How can I plan for tax? Simple - put away what you will pay in terms of tax on *every* invoice you bill - I usually slice off about a third of what I earn and pop it into a satellite account called "tax". That way it grows over the year, and you are fully covered for tax and National Insurance, with some left over. I like to always have a buffer in this account, in case I get a nasty surprise; hence I shift a third of my earnings. This can also act as sick or holiday pay.

It may be worth opening a separate bank account for your everyday needs. I essentially pay myself a day-to-day salary from my earnings account while additionally transferring money from the earnings account into the household account. You may prefer to have it all to come into one account and manage it from there, but do give it some careful thought, and work out a way that ensures you manage your money wisely.

The "easy to ignores": sick pay, holiday pay, barren times, and pensions

When you start off as a freelancer, there is a collection of "easy to ignores" that initially don't feel important. But if you want your freelance salary to take on a fully equivalent status to your previous teacher salary, you need to look at these from the beginning of your journey.

If you get sick as a freelancer, you don't get paid. By the same token, if you take a holiday, you don't get paid. These unpaid days in part will dictate the pay rates that you ask for. So, for example, if you billed at £200/day and worked every working day of the year, that would be a £52,000. I certainly wouldn't turn that down. But say you then take off 25 days and eight bank holidays. That takes you down to a salary of £45,400. Then, let's allow for a maximum of five days sick over the year - you are now down to £44,000. It still feels pretty impressive, but the problem that comes with freelance work is that it is not guaranteed, and in fact just two days a month without work would bring you down under

£40,000. Now for the sting in the tail ... your pension. To continue to have a pension (and remember, it is only you paying in when you are freelance, not an employer), the recommended amount you want to be sacrificing is between ten and 20% of your salary – that's another £4,000-8,000, which now takes our imagined salary down to £32,000-36,000 – the equivalent of a top-end MPR but not on the UPR.

Time off and holiday earnings

This is one I've never fully managed to master. As we have said earlier, if you truly want a week off as a freelancer, you'll simply not get paid. If you have planned for this in your overall earnings, essentially "saving up" for a holiday, that is fine. But if you haven't then it'll be a struggle that month.

Then, of course, there is the issue of telling clients that you are unavailable. I find it really hard to turn work down – I always worry they won't offer again. But if you are in demand, and they've previously given you plenty of work, the chances are they will offer again. I usually approach it by letting all my clients know that I will be off at that time, or if I still need to earn a little, but want some time off, I will tell certain clients I am away and others not. I also use this approach for when I am overloaded. Another tactic I have used is to work the weekends in the build-up to a holiday so that deadlines could be met during the holiday period, without actually having to do the work during that time.

Pensions

Pensions aren't part of the deal when you are freelance, so you need to consider how you are making allowance for this. You will still be paying into National Insurance, so you will have your state pension, but it is worth seeing if you can take out a pension to top up where your teacher pension will have finished off. Otherwise you are not building your pension in any meaningful way.

Non-billable time

Don't forget that time spent sending invoices, tracking and chasing payments, and completing your tax return (usually around half a day, depending on what you do and if you need to go through receipts) is all time that you can't bill for. Also, pitching for work and seeking out projects takes time and energy. Remember to bake this into your week in whatever way works best for you – you may decide to do all admin once a month and have an admin day, or you may prefer to spend a morning or afternoon a week doing it. You may even be able to take care of any admin that arises on the same day.

Pay rises

Remember that your day rate won't go up with inflation unless you put it up. Clients won't suddenly offer you a pay rise. So, in the early days, make sure you have embedded a buffer so that you can sit on your day rate for a couple of years until you feel confident enough to suggest to regular or new clients that your rate has increased. Always do this for new clients and start again at a rate you are happy to sit on for the next couple of years, not what you have already been sitting on for a period of time.

In the ten years I have been freelancing, my hourly rate has increased by 20% – exactly in line with inflation. But be warned that when a client dictates cost per piece or per project, you may need to either do it quicker or haggle a higher rate.

The day-to-day reality of freelance

Working as a freelancer means you are completely in charge of your work. This includes work equipment, your workspace, and your working day, all of which need a remarkable amount of thought.

What equipment will you need?

If you are working as a freelancer, those things that you have previously been "given" with the job will disappear, and you'll need to ensure you have the tools for the job. Things you purchase to do your job are tax-deductible, so do keep receipts and keep track of what you are spending. The chances are you'll need:

- A laptop
- Possibly a cloud subscription if you are going to be creating a lot of work that you need to save and have accessible in different places
- Notebooks (old-fashioned or electronic)
- A desk – see what follows for important aspects of your work set-up

Where and when will you work?

In my early days as a freelancer, this would have seemed a daft question. My answer would have been "at home, of course". And, actually, ten years on I do still work from home, but I also work once a week or fortnight in a London office for my contracted role. Do reflect carefully on the practicalities of your workspace and location:

1. Find someone to talk to – try to make sure you see someone to talk to most days – even Teams calls or the like. Working out of the house and interacting with others will reduce loneliness and help maintain the communication skills that come with day-to-day work interactions

2. Find a couple of different places you like working in the house – I don't have a dedicated desk space, so I often work on the kitchen table or with a lap table on the sofa. I had always read that you should never work in your bedroom, but, actually, it works really well for me and has done for years. I often start work at 04:30 with a coffee in bed and my laptop on a lap tray. That way I can fit in a snuggly, warm two hours before my eldest gets up for school

3. Use an online management system, like Trello, to help organise your priorities. Working for different clients isn't like working for different departments of the same organisation, where people in each department know you are busy on other projects. You need to manage this yourself

4. Still keep a work calendar or diary. It might only be you looking at it, but it saves the time running away from you and helps you to juggle multiple projects at once

5. Try to avoid the kitchen cupboards, and set times for tea-breaks. Imagine you are in an office or at a place of work and stick to your schedule

6. Get outside. When you're not commuting to work, it is very easy to not step out the door for days on end. Eat lunch in the garden or park, or go for a walk or bike ride during your lunch break

7. Book in your lunch break, or it won't happen. The freelance mentality of "if I don't work, I don't earn" can have quite a negative impact on your day-to-day work-life balance

8. Set yourself a time to switch everything off. It helps disconnect work and home

9. Have a few alternatives to your home environment for a workspace. There are plenty of options which won't break the bank:

    - Hot-desking hubs
    - The gym
    - Cafés
    - Community centres
    - The library
    - In someone else's office
    - In someone else's home

Managing and motivating yourself

Motivation outside the classroom is very different from motivation inside the classroom. Suddenly you will find the pressures very different, and, depending on what you end up doing, you may encounter experiences you are not used to:

- Immediate deadlines that require intensive concentration and no flexibility
- Long-term projects that need you to plan your work time carefully to ensure completion

- Several different projects, possibly for different clients or employers, which must be organised simultaneously
- Receiving feedback on written work
- Running workshops or sessions with young people or adults with whom you have no working relationship
- Redrafting work you thought was finished
- Repetition or boredom
- Lots of online meetings

These circumstances will all require a different sort of motivation from that you have been used to. When you shift to a life outside of the classroom, it is really easy to breathe and unburden yourself of the day-to-day stress and pressure of a teacher's life. But any work will bring with it pressure points and expectations which you will have to motivate yourself to meet:

- Ensure you understand and can manage workflow
- Find techniques both to motivate yourself to work and to set work boundaries
- Break your day down into manageable chunks
- Create a routine that reflects your work patterns

You are already really good at managing a nearly impossible workload, but a lot of that is firefighting, and a lot of your working day has previously been dictated to you, as well as being made up of practical and interactive sessions. Leaving the classroom or working outside of the classroom for part of your week can be surprisingly tricky to manage without workflow strategies and tools.

You will have deadlines for expected completion of projects, workshops, and so on, regardless of what work you are doing. In some roles these will continue to be dictated to you, or partly dictated to you, while in other roles you will need to manage them yourself.

1. Understand how long you "should" be spending on a project or task
2. Set out your time budget for projects in blocks or across a period of time
3. Use your calendar to plan your days and weeks
4. Add in wriggle room
5. Learn to say no/not today
6. Set yourself mini goals
7. Be realistic
8. Don't forget admin time
9. Block out your lunchtime/exercise time
10. Set a start and finish time to your day

Managing your workload

Managing your workload can be especially hard when you are freelancing for lots of different people and organisations. Don't be afraid to say you are booked up with other work. If you are good at what you do, then generally you will get booked up, and people in my experience are usually happy to wait. I am always honest and tell them that I can't meet their deadline but could do it at a later time. Nine times out of ten this is agreeable, and when it isn't, I usually follow up with a "but if there is anything else you would like me to do, I have a gap here …".

Sometimes you really want to do a piece of work or project for a number of reasons (kudos, exposure, interest, money … the list goes on), and in these cases you have a few options:

1. Work your weekends – much as I hate to suggest it, especially as an ex-teacher, sometimes this is the only way. And, actually, the mentality is completely different when you are being paid to work your weekend
2. Re-jig some other work – if you know another project has a more arbitrary deadline, that client may be happy to push the deadline back a bit. I generally wouldn't tell them it is because you have other work, but would gently ask if an extension is possible, without going into reasons

I also never take a Friday as a deadline for the simple fact that having a weekend buffer can be a lifesaver. I will often finish something on a Friday and send it, knowing it is due the following Monday, but having the buffer allows you headspace if it needs a check or edit, as well as shuffle room if something comes up in the week that has a tight turnaround.

The joys of freelance

We have explored many aspects of freelance life that may make it seem like the challenge is perhaps not worth the effort. In fact, you may think that I am trying to put you off. Yes, it is a challenge, and, yes, you will need to give many potential pitfalls the due care and consideration they deserve; however, being freelance has many obvious benefits. There are many things I genuinely love, and these have kept me freelancing for so long:

- Picking and choosing work I want
- Working the hours I want to in a permanent flexitime
- Being flexible around a young family
- Exercising when I feel like it
- Catching up with friends during the day
- No commuting costs

- Self-management
- Work where you like
- Develop a range of skill sets
- Treat yourself to a random day off!

The freelance back-up: supply teaching

I'd like to end this chapter by considering one of the key opportunities for making freelancing work. Remember, during barren periods, or as a means to "keep your hand in", supply teaching can be a lifesaver. It is also easier to get and guarantee than other freelance work, especially in the early stages of a move away from the classroom. And remember that if you have a taxing day, you don't have to come back tomorrow (unless you have already agreed to). You also don't have all the administrative and bureaucratic extras to do.

Contact some local schools directly, if you can, and work through the local authority, as the money and benefits are generally better than using supply teaching agencies. Private or independent schools usually, but not always, pay a premium for supply, so that is also worth consideration.

Surviving supply work

Supply teaching can be very challenging, despite the reduced responsibility and the shorter hours, but to make it work well, try to adopt a mindset that will keep bringing you (and the schools you work in) back for more:

- Make sure you work professionally, complete all marking, and leave the absent teacher a clear summary of the day's events, including items that you, as a teacher yourself, know will actually be useful (who really focused/tried hard, any incidents they should know about, anything that didn't work in class, and anything that didn't get finished, or that you did additionally)
- Try to look at a day of supply as a full eight-hour day of work - arrive early to prep and stay afterwards to finish up. Depending on what you do for the day you may end up with a shorter day

Now that you are all set up and raring to go, in the next chapter we explore ways to find work and the how to pitch for freelance projects.

8 Pitching, prodding, and making yourself stand out

So you know what it is you'd like to do, but how on earth do you get there? There are potentially a few routes you may wish to ride, and each one will need a different approach, be it applying for jobs the old-fashioned way, approaching organisations, pitching for work, or marketing your own business.

Going freelance

Going freelance gives you the option to start slowly and on a small scale, perhaps adding in one or two extras while you work, and maybe building to some kind of hybrid role where you teach part-time and freelance the rest of the week. After I had a few freelance clients under my belt – ones that were known in the industry – I found that new pitches and bids for freelance jobs became far easier to win. There is definitely a feeling that, if you have proven your skills, you are more likely to get the gig.

Find your experience

This may seem like an odd thing to suggest: surely you either have experience or you don't? Actually, as teachers you have a lot more experience than you may realise; for example, you will likely have the following experience as a writer:

- Writing lesson plans, creating resources, writing samples for students
- Writing policies
- Writing action plans, risk assessments, budget requests
- Writing emails and letters (home and internally)
- Writing newsletters or blogs
- Writing school reports

Identify your skills and experiences and reflect on your strengths.

Develop your experience

Whatever it is you want to do, you'll need to not only show you have the skills, but make sure you develop those skills. If, for example, you want to write articles or create education content, then, as with everything else, you need to practise. Start out by writing a blog for yourself or for school, creating really great

DOI: 10.4324/9781003378334-8

resources for school, or writing for your school newsletter. Writing in a voluntary capacity is a great way to get experience (especially if you can get some feedback), but do be wary of commercial firms or publications expecting you to write for free, especially when they are making money out of it. Exposure and experience are great; exploitation is not.

Learn to pitch

To build up freelance work, you are most likely going to need to pitch for it, whether that is pitching in the traditional sense or putting in speculative applications. Each pitch needs to be organisation- and role-specific. Pitching is essentially selling your ideas (rather than fully formed offerings) for articles, resources, or other project work. It is a creative process, and, much like an author keeps a notebook of ideas, it is good practise to keep a notebook (electronic or real) for things you read or ideas that come to you. The more current, relevant, interesting, and unique you can make your ideas, the better. For example, if there has been a lot in the press of late around teacher workloads, you might decide to pitch for:

- A simple toolkit
- Tips for keeping the focus in place
- Time management hints and tips
- An article on how to say "no" or "not now"!
- A teacher's guide to switching off
- CPD or workshop sessions around reducing workloads

Always include a brief but informative covering email that tells the recipient why they should publish this idea (an offer of statistics you have seen, or a summary of how much front-page coverage the issue has received) and why you should be the author – tell them about your extensive experience and that you have already written for others (even if it's for employers), or direct them to a blog, if you have one. Include a one-page CV that sets out key experiences and links to any work you have published. And don't be disheartened if you don't get the gig or if they plain old ignore you. Keep pushing, and you will get there in the end.
As a general rule of thumb:

- Identify who you want to pitch to and why – do your research to find the right person to contact, and see if you can connect with them on LinkedIn, as this usually gives you contact details
- Don't write an article or create a resource in full before someone has agreed to publish it, but do have samples of your writing available, preferably online
- Do send your ideas to several places – more than one of them may well want to pick it up, but waiting on them one at a time will take months

- Don't write too much in a covering email, or they will switch off - just tell them what they need to know
- Do be bold and send several different ideas in one email - provide a summary of each idea; one may jump out, and you have your hook in
- Do try to have a positive spin, if you are writing an article on an education issue. Lots of publications are looking for insightful but inspiring pieces rather than negative pieces
- Always offer a short biographical paragraph and a clear indication of what your email is about
- Know how long things will take, what your hourly rate will be, and how you will negotiate, but don't mention money up front

Finding contacts and building networks

With a little work building contacts and networks is very achievable, and LinkedIn now offers an easy and transparent way to find and connect with the right people. Always do some digging around, using simple searches: "commissioning editor [name of organisation or publication]".

If you are not sure they are the right person, say that up front in your email, and ask them to please forward it to the right person. I commonly receive a response from the addressee, saying they have passed it on and offering me the correct contact details so that I can follow up.

Once you have established a working relationship with organisations or individuals, have the confidence to continue to pitch new ideas but also to always offer to take any commissions they may have coming up. Do this every now and again, as commissioning editors and content creators are often under great pressure, and if you pop up at just the right moment, you may find a commission landing in your inbox. With any pitching or commissioning, you do need to be prepared for them to jump at your offer and ask for the product next week. I never pitch an article if I can't deliver it within a week.

Blow your own trumpet!

As you build your freelance experience, you'll find that it starts to work in your favour. If one known company is paying you to freelance, then others will follow suit. You won't be asked for samples as much. You'll also find that, over time, some commissioning editors you work with become more open to you contacting them about available work. They'll also start emailing you to ask if they can commission you. Remember Gaiman's three key hotspots: be nice to work with, always meet deadlines, and produce work of a high quality.

If you are applying speculatively, make them think they need you, even though they may not realise it initially. Tell them what you are offering and the positive impact it could have for them (without suggesting they need to be "saved"). Your confidence will come across and give them the confidence to take a chance on you.

Employment outside of the classroom

A new role or a part-time split

Many teachers just want a change, and applying for new jobs - whether part-time, alongside a reduced teaching role, or full-time as a completely new direction - may be the route for them. A few things will need consideration:

- Notice periods
- Showing how you have the skills for a role that isn't teaching
- The age/experience bias

Notice periods

It may seem obvious but teaching notice periods are not short, and, in fact, many teachers prefer to leave at the end of an academic year; but what if that dream job you want is advertised in November, and they want you to start asap? It's a tricky one, and I have been on both sides of the coin - trying to recruit ex-teachers in a timely fashion and seeing roles appear that I simply couldn't start for a few months.

Employers will often stipulate that they'd like teaching experience, which can lull jobbing teachers into a false sense of security around lead-in times, but the reality is that many of these employers will want candidates to start sooner than later. Some may have their act together and be recruiting early enough for school notice periods, but most won't, even for the elusive "stand-out" candidate.

Often the "teaching" candidates that get the job have, in fact, already given notice or left the profession and are working short contracts or supply teaching. This is a riskier tactic, but one that makes you more attractive. I had given notice on a teaching role twice before a shift into non-classroom-based roles - in fact, on both occasions I had given notice a good while before the end of the year so that I could openly tell my head when I had interviews. She appreciated being able to fill the role with plenty of notice. You need to be in a place of financial stability, though. The alternative is to intensify job searches close to your notice period and to accept that you might lose your summer holiday. You should give notice by no later than:

- 31st October to leave on 31st December
- 28th February to leave on 30th April
- 31st May to leave on 31st August (this would actually feel more like seven weeks' notice)

Applying for a role that isn't teaching

When we look at non-teaching roles that ask for teaching experience, it is really easy to fall into the trap of blowing our teaching trumpet and losing sight of the actual role and the array of skills it demands. Often when we see that a role requires teaching experience, our go-to is to wave a flag and highlight that we are a teacher. It is really important that we do this, but we must also ensure we apply for the actual job on offer and look at all the asks for the role. Remember, all applicants will be teachers, so you'll need to stand out.

Look at this (fictional) example of a job ad:

> Creative, knowledgeable, and experienced education writer needed, with an eye for detail and exceptional writing skills. We are looking for a qualified teacher with a minimum of five years classroom experience. You should have held a subject leader role for at least two years and be able to demonstrate understanding of effective classroom and subject management. With a keen interest in the education landscape, you will be expected to demonstrate sound research skills and an ability to cut through the detail and summarise news stories and research reports and publications. A team player, you will also have the ability to work alone and have a flexible approach to work.

Teaching experience is required, but the role is a writing post, and the company is a commercial one. You need to not only apply for the role advertised but convince the employer that you really want to work for their organisation, as opposed to no longer wanting to remain in your current job. It is a subtle difference, but one that potential employers can sniff out a mile off. Don't tell them why you want to leave the classroom but, rather, why you want this role, and why you want to want to work for them. Focus on the pull of the job rather than the push of the classroom.

Break down what you are being asked for into bullet points, so that you can identify what they want and how you fit the mark:

- Creative education writer
- Knowledgeable education writer
- Experienced education writer
- An eye for detail

- Exceptional writing skills
- Qualified teacher with a minimum of five years classroom experience
- Subject leader role for at least two years
- Understanding of effective classroom and subject management
- Interest in the education landscape
- Sound research skills
- Ability to cut through the detail and summarise news stories and research reports and publications
- A team player
- Can work alone
- Flexible approach to work

There is a lot there, but employers are going to want to see that you can meet their criteria, as well as that you have done your homework and can identify why you specifically want to work for them as an organisation. Part-time education roles like these are few and far between and can be highly competitive – you may find yourself up against over 100 candidates, meaning anyone who doesn't tick all the boxes will be on the discard pile very fast.

Start any application by creating a table and filling in all the possible ways you can fulfil the criteria. Then compose some sentences that summarise each box to help write your covering letter and CV. Have a look at the example in Figure 8.1.

	Experience	Summary
Creative education writer	• Written creative resources and content for the classroom • Freelance activity-idea articles for education publication • Currently write school blog • Currently write my own education blog	I am an experienced and creative writer of classroom content and education-focused articles.
Knowledgeable education writer	• Written articles on current education issues • Written school policies • Currently write school blog • Currently write my own education blog	I follow and write about the current education landscape in my own blog on education issues.

Figure 8.1 Sample job application chart

	Experience	Summary
Experienced education writer	• Three years freelance writing for various education publications • Writing policies, plans, resources etc in school for seven years • Own blog for two years	I have been writing for over seven years in many different formats.
An eye for detail	• Edit own work • Mark pupil work • Write accurate pupil reports to go out to parents • Currently write school blog and my own blog	I have a good eye for detail, editing my own and other colleagues' reports in school.
Exceptional writing skills	• Several articles published in education publications	I regularly write for …
Qualified teacher with a minimum of five years classroom experience	• Spent seven years in classroom (KS1 and KS2)	I am an experienced teacher, with over seven years' classroom experience.
Subject leader role for at least two years	• History and geography subject lead for four years • Pastoral lead and KS2 lead for two years	I have successfully led history and geography for four years and consider myself an expert in these subjects. I additionally have experience as a pastoral lead across KS2.
Understanding of effective classroom and subject management	• Outstanding teacher • Recent subject deep dive suggested outstanding management and practise • KS2 lead includes CPD and mentoring of staff in classroom management	I have been described as an outstanding practitioner and key stage leader. I regularly run subject-specific CPD and mentor staff.
Interest in the education landscape	• My personal blog • Subscribe to several education update sites • Subscribe to Schools Week	I keep abreast of the education landscape and write regularly on current issues in my blog.

Figure 8.1 (Continued)

	Experience	Summary
Sound research skills	• Completed action research on humanities in primary schools • I regularly research articles for publication	I completed action research in the classroom on humanities in primary schools and regularly contribute articles for publication that require considered research on the current education landscape.
Ability to cut through the detail and summarise news stories and research reports and publications	• Disseminate information to keep staff up-to-date	As subject lead, I run a monthly humanities-update meeting, where I disseminate the key things teachers need to know.
A team player	• With KS2 lead and subject leads – across different teams	I work effectively across KS2 as lead and am a team player when it comes to subject leadership, guiding but also working with year group teams to achieve successful outcomes.
Can work alone	• First role was single-form entry • Subject lead	I have also worked in a single-form entry school, where, while collaboration with other teachers was evident, my own planning needed to be developed in isolation.
Flexible approach to work	• In juggling so many balls, I have to be flexible and versatile	As a teacher, key stage lead, and subject lead, I am adept at keeping several balls in the air at once!

Figure 8.1 (Continued)

Write a bespoke covering letter

Potential employers know when you have sent them a "catch-all" covering letter, mainly because it doesn't really say much about the role or their organisation. By creating a job-application chart, like in Figure 8.1, you are essentially creating the basis of your covering letter in terms of the role. Add to this a clear understanding of the organisation you are applying to and a convincing rationale for why you want to work for them, and you have a bespoke covering letter that will likely get you past the initial CV cull.

Do also remember that a future employer isn't really interested in your family life or in how this job will help you manage your life better. The job should be valued for the job alone (even if the truth is that it will help you juggle). Employers also don't want to know about how exhausting teaching is or how disillusioned you are. They would rather understand that you are excited by a new challenge that brings all of your experiences to bear in a new role. They'll want to know what value you can add to the team and role, and that you won't jump straight back into the classroom when the going gets tough.

Update your CV

You are going to need to update your CV to accompany your covering letter. Applying for a non-classroom role is very different from applying for a teaching post, so there is every chance that this is the first CV you have written in a long while. Make sure that your CV is clearly tailored for the education role you are applying for, and that the recruiter doesn't feel like they are looking at a repackaged teacher. They need to see a candidate with teaching experience.

- Include the most relevant experiences, and block bits together if needed
- Make sure your skill set is convincing and relevant to the role
- Take time to inform the recruitment team that you actually want the role and why you are the perfect candidate
- Prove your skills

What to expect from the recruitment process: tasks and interviews

Once your covering letter and CV have got you through to the next stage, you will likely need to prove yourself beyond just an interview (and there may well be more than one round of interviews). In the same way you are asked to teach a lesson for a teaching post, you may be asked to complete a task. For example, in the past I have been asked to complete written tasks, reading tasks, presentations, and sample-ideas documents.

The interview process may also feel very different. Think carefully about what you want to share, and have some good examples to back up your skills or scenarios. Think carefully about possible pinch points in the new role for which you feel like you lack experience – these pinch points will be different from those in teaching, but you will have comparable skills:

Clients = parents

Written communication = school reports and planning documents

Collaboration = year group partners, subject leadership

Working with and managing relationships with senior staff = being on the SLT

Project management = school trips, running staff meetings, running a classroom, and the learning therein

The age/experience bias

If you are very experienced and have been teaching for a long while, it is possible your CV could give the impression that you've become a teaching fossil. Some employers can be put off by decades of teaching experience – they may think that you are less malleable and may cost more. We also read a lot about the barriers over-50s experience when applying for jobs, but there are ways to use this to your advantage.

Yes, you are more expensive, and yes, you may not have grown up in the digital age, but that only shows how adaptive you are. You will likely be pretty tech-savvy, having worked in schools, and you will also know your audience if you go on to do something education-related. There are a few things you can do to make your experience feel less like a mountain for prospective employers and more like a scenic stroll:

- Clump experiences where appropriate: e.g. *I taught across the primary phase in three different schools from 2008-2019*
- Make each experience stand out for a unique reason, and explain how it improved your skills base or flexibility: e.g. *class teacher, subject lead, year group or KS lead, CPD lead*
- Be ready to explain more carefully why you want to move after so many years

Remember, you may be up against applicants with less time in the classroom, who are not as expensive as you and who, in fact, may be more attractive to employers who see them as more malleable. But they won't have as many experiences as you, and you will need to make this work in your favour.

9 So you want to run your own business …

Applying for a new role or pitching for freelance work is one thing, but what if you want to run your own business? While there is a distinction between freelance and being self-employed, the line is blurry. Technically, if you work freelance, you tend to work for other people and organisations to create products or provide services that they usually claim as their own. Starting your own business is a whole different ballgame, and while it seems an attractive option, it is one to be entertained with caution. Running your own business will take a lot of time and energy, and you will need to learn a lot along the way. And unless you can afford to go without earning for an indefinite period, your business may need to be a side hustle that grows as your teaching career shrinks.

The reality of running your own business

In 2019, a teacher friend and I launched Subject Leaders,[1] a service for subject leads in primary schools. We research news, competitions, funding, CPD, and all things going on in each National Curriculum subject and add this information to one of 12 dedicated subject pages on our website, sending out a monthly update to our subscribers. Sounds pretty straightforward, and, yes, the concept is, but the reality is that there is a lot going on in the background, from website and back-end management to marketing and finances. But if you believe in your product or service, and have the capacity to take this route, setting up and running your own business can be a very rewarding and very viable option.

Know what you want to do

While your new business venture doesn't have to be focused on education, it does make a lot of sense to take your education know-how to create a new product or service that you feel you have expertise in. The key to starting any business is identifying an effective idea for your audience, which is simple and focused. Consider the following questions when deciding what you'd like to do:

- What is your idea and why would it work?
- Does someone else already do this, and, if they do, are you a direct or indirect competitor? Is there enough space for all of you?

DOI: 10.4324/9781003378334-9

- Are you focusing on teachers in the classroom or senior leaders buying in for their school?

There is an array of potential routes you could take, with some of the more common education businesses falling into some clear-cut categories.

Tutoring business

Whether a one-person show or a multi-tutor company, you'll need to be confident with your approach, your stretch, and your specialisms. Parents who pay for tutoring often have a specific expectation: passing national exams, passing entrance exams, shifting into top-level attainment. You need to be confident with what you are doing and able to be realistic with parents.

Curriculum planning business

This is big business these days. Some companies or offerings, like Plan B, Kapow, or Hamilton Trust, cover an array of subjects, while others, such as Oddizzi, Language Angels, or Literacy Shed, are single-subject focused. If you are strong on one area and have the right qualifications and background, then this may be a great option. If you want to create a commercial scheme, you'll really need to know your subject well and understand the intricacies of how it is planned, taught, and learnt. With the scrutiny of Ofsted, anything less just won't succeed.

Classroom or teacher resources business

Is there something that you are convinced will make life easier in the classroom, or that you know teachers won't be able to resist? Creating a story-bags business or a teacher-focused stationery business, for example, may be niche, but if you have an audience for whom it works, these kinds of resources could be the making of a successful business.

An education service

Consultancy and CPD training will need years of experience to back up your status, but if this is what you have, schools will likely be happy to pay for your services. Understanding the world of education from a grassroots perspective may also set you up to offer a support service for schools, such as Subject Leaders.

Clubs business

Many schools will happily advertise for external clubs, but make sure you have insurance and have thought through the resources and expectations you have.

Parents will always love a club that is run by ex-teachers and especially one that develops skills (sport, languages, arts etc).

Do your homework

Once you have identified what your business will be, you'll need to start laying the foundations and identifying your needs. Some of the things you'll need to consider include:

- Where to find your audience and how to market your business to them
- The landscape – what is the competition and what will make your service or product different
- Upfront costs
- Day-to-day running costs and commitments (remember that your time is a cost, even if you are not earning initially)
- Any external expertise you are going to need
- How to build a website
- How to develop an online presence

Find a partner

A problem shared is a problem halved. Actually, the same can often be said of a business partner. If you can find one who has the same passion for your idea as you do and is someone who you are confident you can work alongside, then having a business partner certainly makes it easier when it comes to divvying up the tasks and making decisions. They will also prove to be a creative force and will help you to develop ideas and concepts.

Developing the right skills

The chances are that if you are starting an education-focused business, you are bringing the key expertise and skills that will sit at the core of the business and will give it a certain level of credibility. However, you will need to wear countless hats when running a business, and there will be many aspects you won't have a clue about or only have limited experience in. When starting Subject Leaders, my business partner and I found that the key skills, experience, and expertise that we needed were:

- Content writing
- Research
- Web management
- Marketing

- Communications
- Finances
- Design
- Editing
- Customer service
- Social media
- Project management

Some of these additional skills won't suit you, but many will develop and grow as your business grows. Some you will need to muddle through and work out for yourself; some you will want or need to get some training in; and others you will simply need to find and employ in those skill sets. Figure 9.1 sets out my skills set before starting Subject Leaders and then four years into the journey. While I am still not destined for a career in finance, my skills set is now much more in line with the business need, thanks to trial and error, exposure, and self-development. You can also see where my partner's skills set complements mine. We still have external design, website, and editorial support, and we pay an accountant to sort out our annual tax return, but the rest we do ourselves.

Skill/role		Skills set/experience 1 (low) – 10 (high)									
		1	2	3	4	5	6	7	8	9	10
Content writing											
Research											
Web management											
Marketing											
Comms											
Finances											
Design											
Editing											
Customer service											
Social media											
Project management											

	Additional fill-in skill from my business partner		Skills prior to Subject Leaders		Skills after four years of Subject Leaders

Figure 9.1 Skills set prior to Subject Leaders and after four years of running the business

Price yourself sensibly

How will you cost your product or service? Remember that schools have little in the way of budget and are bombarded on a daily basis by products and services. But you also don't want to under-price your product or service, as this gives the impression that it isn't up to standard. Do some research and find some similar businesses. How much do they cost? Be as competitive as you can without undervaluing what you have on offer. Remember, if you are bottling 20 years of experience, the price on the label needs to reflect this. People are paying for your expertise.

Call in as many favours as you can

If you know people who could help out or are happy to do "mate's rates", bring them in. Don't take advantage, and ensure that you go back to them once you are up and running, making it a more lucrative offer of help in the first place. For Subject Leaders, we had close family members with design and editorial skills who wanted to help us launch. We also had a friend who worked in web development who was keen to get involved and charged his services at cost, and a friend who was a subject specialist in an area we couldn't cover. We rewarded all of these people for their time, either financially or in other ways.

Marketing and communications: finding your voice

It's a tricky one but worth trying for yourself initially, as you are likely to have the contacts and know where to go. Don't be drawn in by very expensive advertising, as the chances are it won't work. Do your homework on UK General Data Protection Regulation (GDPR) before you embark on any email campaigns, and learn how to email effectively. There are online courses, or, even better, think about those emails you receive that make you open up and click through. What do they do and why does it work?

You'll also need to think carefully about your comms voice, and the tone you want to project. Imagine your business has a personality. How do you want people to describe it? You need to find your voice, tone, and personality, and build your brand around that. Will it be:

- Friendly and chatty
- No-nonsense and relaxed
- Gentle and quietly professional
- Formal and highly professional

You are in a unique position, as you are your audience or client, and so you have insider information on the voice that is needed or wanted. Teachers like to know it is one of their own helping them out – someone who understands their needs, someone who understands classroom management or school needs, someone who understands that they are tired, and someone who genuinely wants to help and knows how to help. The "been there, done that" status that comes with being ex-teacher counts for a lot in the education-business world, so make sure you present this through the voice of your business.

Commit for the long haul

Businesses aren't generally overnight successes but need time to grow. You need to be realistic about how long it may take to start making money and may also need to set a limit on how long you will continue with the venture before admitting defeat. The latter is actually harder than the former.

Commit to celebrate the wins and learn from the fails

Don't be too disheartened when things go wrong. Learn from them and move on. Don't be afraid to adapt your business or change its trajectory, if this feels more in tune with your audience needs and your capacity. You may also find you need to adapt based on the level of commitment needed to run the business, especially in the early stages of your business, if you are still earning a salary elsewhere. By the same token, make sure you celebrate the small wins to keep your focus and positivity. Identify what you have achieved and how you have evolved.

Know your limits

When we first came up with the idea for Subject Leaders, the plan for the website was ridiculous, and our ambition to take over the education world was somewhat delusional. However, our website designer helped us to understand our limitations while helping us to realise our ambition in the form of a phase one (we are currently on phase three, after four years of trading). We also hadn't quite anticipated how much work would go into launch – an empty website is not a helpful way to launch a business; rather, it needs to feel fully up and running and functioning. It also needs maintenance, and things go wrong and need updating. You'll need to establish a process for maintenance and updates that works.

Know what you can and what you cannot do. What a shame it would be to create an amazing pile of content for a website that just looks a bit homemade. If website design is something you can do, that's a bonus, but if it isn't, then do not under any circumstances try it alone. Our web developer was a friend, and while we obviously paid for his services, he was kind to us and would often help out every now and again. Expertise comes at a cost, but it is worth every penny.

Earning a salary

You may wonder why the last thing we are considering in this chapter is earning a salary, when the whole point of running a business is to make a living. The reality is that you will likely still need to be working to earn a living when you start a business, as you are unlikely to make an instant profit. However, this causes a conflict, as the business would thrive more if you could put work into it every day. You may even find yourself working full time and running a business, which won't be easy. Running a business is a challenging choice and you'll need to be prepared to work hard and overcome the frustrations of not being able to dedicate 100% of your time to it. But if there is a need for your product or service, and if you believe in and are excited by it, then it'll be worth the effort as your business grows and your profits eventually bring you a salary.

In the next chapter we look at ways to build your online persona and how social media is a key tool for any freelance work or business.

Note

1   www.subjectleaders.co.uk.

10 Building your online persona

Social media in a freelance world

Embracing social media can be key to success in the world of freelance. Knowing how to create your own handles and how to use different social media forms to share your expertise or to build networks and knowledge are all part of the process.

The power of social media can be your friend when it comes to freelance work or running your own business, but before you launch into running your own social media empire, you need to give some careful consideration to your set-up and plan in detail how you will run your accounts:

- Your handle name
- Your handle look and feel
- Whom you will follow
- What kinds of things you will share or retweet
- How you can connect with your audience
- What you offer for free that will build followers

Essentially you need to see yourself as a brand - something that has a clear purpose and audience. You need to think carefully about what that purpose is, how you want to come across, what you'd like to be known for, and who your target audience is. You also need to consider if you are becoming a "teacher" brand (known or unknown), an education skill or area brand, or a business brand that sits in education.

Which platforms should you use?

Each social media platform is different in terms of its audience but also the manner in which it tends to be used. You may decide to have accounts across all platforms or may prefer to focus on one or two. But before you start, make sure you understand the platforms you intend to use. If you have never touched Instagram, I wouldn't recommend rocking up and announcing your arrival without understanding how it works and how people tend to interact on it. The best way to gain an understanding is by being on it and creating a personal profile to start with - keep it private so that you can get a feel for the form.

DOI: 10.4324/9781003378334-10

(Edu)Twitter tends to be more about the sharing of ideas and links. It is useful if you want to follow for information or share ideas, links, and news in a more formal context.

Instagram is all about the pictures. It is a very accessible and visual form of social media.

LinkedIn is a great place to get networking with people who may help boost your presence online, but also, if you are trying to promote yourself or a business in a work context, this is definitely a key platform. Don't be frightened to reach out to people you don't know – if you are in education and they are in education, they will often link-in, as networking works both ways.

Facebook is great for interactions, especially on subject groups or specialist groups. Facebook ads are also highly effective if you are selling a service or product, as they can be super cheap (you set your budget) and can reach quite a large and specific (teacher) audience. You will also likely have lots of friends with friends who may be happy to share your posts, meaning they spread quicker than on the other social media sites.

Your handle

Your purpose will and should influence your handle name. You may wish to set up a "business" account in your own name, create a pseudonym or role-based name, or, if it is for your own business, use your company name. Whichever it is, the name needs to be memorable and relatable and to do what it says on the tin – nothing too cryptic. There are a multitude of education handles that are clearly named for what they do and offer:

- Mr T does Primary History (Stuart Tiffany)
- Maths Jem (Jo Morgan)
- Those that can (Dr Emma Kell)

Think carefully about what you call yourself, and try to be consistent across the board. If you are still working in schools, you may prefer to use a pseudonym and not place your image on things. Alternatively you may want to use your position to your favour. Do talk to your headteacher, though, to ensure you are within contract. It could likely have a positive impact on your school and its status, but there are also some potential pitfalls to be cognisant of:

Pros

- Can promote the reputation of your school
- Can raise the profile of your school
- Can show that you are the real deal

Cons

- If it goes wrong, it could get you into a lot of trouble
- The school reputation could be at stake
- You will have to stick to the safe stuff and not put out anything too controversial
- You may want to avoid sharing too much of your personal life, as your students will most likely come across your account

Your look and feel

There are plenty of free images out there to help with design (please make sure they are copyright-free – places like Pixabay offer free-to-use images). When you think about the look and feel, consider these questions:

- Do you want your face out there or would you prefer to hide behind a design?
- What is the message and brand purpose you need to project?
- How will you ensure that your accomplishments elicit kudos to what you say?

Remember, one look at your profile will tell others about you, and this is your main way to get yourself out there and noticed.

Your purpose

Social media is a door to sharing your "purpose" – essentially the personality of the work you want to do. Think about the key messages you'd like to share and how you can present that on social media. You will likely want to present one of three purposes and their accompanying "personalities":

- **Welcome to my world of teaching** - do you want to come across as friendly and human? Will people follow you because you are relatable and funny in a "colleague in the next classroom" kind of way? Do you want to share your life as a teacher?
- **Subject authority** - do you want to be an authority and the "go-to" person for a subject or area?
- **Education specialist** – do you want to become an authority on education issues of the day?

Running your social media accounts

Connecting with your audience

Once you are all set up, you need to then consider what you are going to post and how you are going to engage with your audience.

- Do some homework and find people you admire who have proven successful online in your area in a way that you would like to be
- Find things that are of interest to your audience, and repost or create your own posts around this
- Be careful with your comments and observations at the outset, as social media can be a harsh playing ground and you don't want to appear too controversial while you build followers
- Make sure everything in your post has correct spelling, punctuation, and grammar. This is especially important for the education world
- Add an image to your posts that your audience can relate to and that feels familiar
- Make your audience feel like they want to agree with you and you are on their side
- Set your boundaries and define who you are so that your audience doesn't become confused. If, for example, you follow someone for their gardening advice and pictures, if they suddenly start putting personal tips on fixing cars on their handles, you may quickly disengage
- Sharing a bit of who you are may work in your favour, but think about what you want out there available for all to see

You want people in your community who help grow your "brand" and nourish what you are doing. In an ideal world they will be sharing your ideas and links. In a perfect world you will be engaging with the big hitters in your "area," which will greatly increase your reach. Have a good think though about what that community is and how you will stand out and "lead" within it.

Whom will you follow?

Whom you follow says a lot about you and may influence people who in turn choose to follow you. Try to engage with people who hold the same values as you and who may help build your reputation or brand. Reply to posts, tag people in posts, recommend others who you genuinely would like to be associated with. Curate a set of people who represent you and your philosophy or brand, as well as those you want to promote yourself to and those who may well post things that help you in your role, service, product you are selling, or personal brand. Consider following:

- People who might be able to help you grow
- People who can give you helpful, insightful, and useful information
- Friends who can help boost your shares and likes

Networking

The key to getting noticed and building a following is networking. You can do this in a number of ways:

1. Identify people you want to network with and follow them
2. Reshare and like things that people you want to network with are sharing
3. Tag in people or organisations you want to network with on relevant posts – probably ones about them. You may want to make sure there is a bit of flattery or praise going on, and preferably in such a way that they will want to re-share what you have said
4. If you find something someone has created, written, or done, it is worth celebrating that online and tagging them on the post. Highlighting something you are finding helpful, interesting, or enjoyable will often lead the author to "love" the post
5. Follow people you want to feed from, as well as those you want to connect with. If you know someone always posts about things of use to you, use this as a way to build up your knowledge
6. Whom do the people you follow, follow? You can often find new people by keeping a close eye on others' followers
7. Be careful to know enough about whomever you are resharing or liking. Keep away from potential controversy

Finding ways to engage on a personal level

People tend to engage more with you if they feel not only that they can relate to you but that you care about them and engage with them in a way that feels personal. Think about some of the things you can do to achieve this:

*   Thank people for following you, by celebrating milestones
*   Thank people for signing up to your service or product. FOMO (fear of missing out) is alive and well, and if people think others are signing up, it will get their curiosity going
*   Celebrate anniversaries – how long have you been on a platform, or how long has your business been running?
*   Share testimonials or praise from people you work with – it shows that people like what you do
*   Share relevant celebration days and tell others what you are up to for that day
*   Share anything you get published – not only will it boost the viewings of the publication, but it will also boost your credibility
*   Run competitions – ones that aren't too off-putting. Make the prize real and something that shows you understand the needs of your audience: a care package for teachers, a free membership or product

Posting on social media

Share things of interest and relevance

If people are following you for your subject or teaching expertise, make sure that is what you give them. Unless it fits well (for example, sharing your gardening adventures while being a teacher expert on science, environmental science, or sustainability works; or sharing travels and visits while being a geography expert), don't mix it up – people who are following you for your art-education expertise are going to find it odd when you start adding in posts about your hobby as an extreme runner. Keep that for a different handle – one that draws in runners!

Make your own videos

Make sure to mix it up a bit when it comes to the format of what you are posting. People like watching videos, especially if they help them in some way that is quick and effective. If you are making videos for expertise, make them practical and immediately implementable. If you are making videos for humour, make sure they are actually funny.

Offer "safe" recommendations

On our Subject Leaders handle, we often share books we are reading to our children at home or in class – this is a safe but very human way of engaging with followers. You may have encountered a new resource, book, video, or course that will be of use to others. People will follow you if they think they get good ideas out of you.

Make your posts eye-catching

Try to incorporate design features that will make your posts stand out. Images (always check the copyright), sound, and visuals go a long way to attracting attention, as does embracing the likes of stories and video effects on Instagram. Consider sharing educational content with Instagram slides.

Add in humour where appropriate

Sometimes there are memes and videos that we just have to share because they hit the nail on the head. Unless you want to be known for this, don't overdo it, but showing a human side every now and again can make you seem more approachable and relatable.

Validity

Only share opinion and advice if you know it is 100% kosher and valid. Know that you can back up your thoughts, and be confident that they are not just a rant or based on false news.

Be the first

When reports and the like come out, teachers love a summary. If you really know your stuff and are confident that you can make a clear and accurate summary of a review or report, be that person who creates and shares it. Put it on relevant pages and groups, and tag people who you think will share.

Use hashtags

Hashtags are highly effective in the education world, especially when it comes to something "in the know". Whenever you post, use hashtags to ramp up views. Bog standard ones (#teachers, #KS3, #EYFS) are helpful, but so are specific ones (#ofstedartreview)

Have a weekly hook

@penny_ten puts out a weekly jobs-in-education update on Twitter every Sunday morning. It is really simple but very effective. If people know you can offer them something for nothing that they find extremely helpful, it will bring them in. At Subject Leaders we put out a weekly "dates for the diary", which is really simple yet hugely popular. Why not post:

- A weekly thought
- Your top-five news articles from the week
- Favourite resources of the week
- The best teacher-packed lunch of the week
- A teacher/education meme of the week

Make sure you stay active and organised

If you want social media to work in your favour, you need to stay active online. If you have followers, they will want to hear from you regularly. Having a weekly update for something, as well as some more laid-back shares, will remind people you are there. Create an editorial schedule so that you know what you will post when, and while it is important to post in reaction to things happening in the education (or any other) world, it is always worth having content written in advance and ready to go.

Other ways to boost your online persona

Let's talk about blogs

Blogs are a great way to raise your online profile and to make yourself interesting and helpful to others. Blog-writing can easily end up being quite bland, though, and often a burden for the author who has committed to writing regularly. To make a blog successful, make sure it is relevant, useful, interesting, and brief. A bad blog won't get read and, even worse, may put people off. A good (and regular) blog is a great thing to pop onto your social media; it draws people into your website and helps them buy into whatever it is you are "selling", whether it is a service, your expertise, or a product.

Blogs can also be cathartic, and if that is your aim, then having readers and followers is less of an issue. But if you want your blog to become your main event, it needs to be useful and appealing. It also needs to be well written and not take an age to read. Make sure you craft your blog with care and get someone trusted to edit it.

Consider carefully the "personality" of your blog and what its purpose is:

- Are you writing from the heart about your education experiences?
- Are you focused on education musings in general?
- Are you focused on a subject or specialism?
- Are you trying to promote your product or services?
- Are you writing on a theme that follows the calendar?
- Are you sharing your professional experiences?
- Are you blogging about others' resources, courses (CPD), services?

Try and define what your blog is and what it is trying to achieve. If you jump around too much, you will confuse your readers, and they may well disengage.

Let's talk about websites

Your website will be the landing page for many of your followers and potential clients or employers, so make sure it sends the messages you want it to. Are you selling yourself (so to speak), a service, a product, or a lifestyle/community? Your website will be the first port of call for any organisation looking to commission you for freelance work, so make sure you showcase any work you have previously done and connect to any projects or organisations you are currently working for. But try to also make your website do something more than just promote you. People want to come to a website for a reason. Host a blog (a good one); set up a calendar; add in links to interesting sites, resources, and reviews; sell your product.

Consider your longevity

Future employers, clients, and freelance prospects will all look you up online, and if you are putting yourself out there, your profile will be readily available for one and all to look at. I can't tell you the number of times I have put a pitch in, spoken to a potential client, or applied for a gig or job and the person at the other end has made it very clear they have read something I have written or have seen things I have posted online. For this reason I am a cautious social media user – if you want to be controversial or to have a clear line of opinion, and if that works well for you and matches your aims, then it is important to focus on that. But in the early stages, and if you want to ensure that you don't alienate potential contacts, make sure you take a go-slow, go-cautious approach. I have seen too many people lose followers at a rate of knots, all because they commented on something in a controversial way, and it is all too easy to do when we are tired, frustrated, or, worse, feel attacked. Always pause before you respond and consider the worst-case-scenario impact. Be careful that what you say can't be misconstrued – the online world is brutal.

By the same token, if you don't want to become too niche, don't present a niche persona online. For example, if you only ever post about maths teaching or assessment processes but then decide you want a job where you are asked to show a passion for sustainability, being narrowly defined online could work against you. By all means have a focus, just be aware of your public face. Of course it can work hugely in your favour: if you have been tweeting and instagramming about student wellbeing for months or years, and this is where your expertise or service lies, then this will help build your credibility and status. You would also stand out as a job applicant in this area if you can show this has been your passion for a long time.

Posting on social media can also help keep you on your game. If you are not committed to posting, then you may manage to keep on top of everything, but if you want to come over as an authority by reading up on everything you can, while sharing and commenting, doing so will keep a lot of current thinking and trends in your head and is a great way of tracking and documenting media and research in your field.

Using social media effectively not only promotes you and builds your reputation; it is also a great way to engage with your audience and potential clients. Well-run and successful social media handles are always carefully thought through, consistent, and engaging – take time to ensure your social media accounts sit within this category.

11 Shifting outside the classroom

It is surprisingly hard to effectively become an ex-teacher. Whether you are making a full shift into freelance education, shifting into part-time work or part-time freelance work, starting a new job, or running your own business, there is a lot to learn about how to shift from life in a classroom to work in the outside world.

Shifting your mindset

When you stop teaching, it takes a while to make the mental shift away from the classroom. Depending on what you do and the direction you take, you may still be connected to the world of education and what is going on in the classroom. You may even still be teaching in a different context. But the key is that you are no longer a teacher, and the pressures and stresses of that role need to become something of the past. You will have new pressures, stresses, and challenges, and will need to embrace these to ensure you make the shift successfully in your head as well as in reality.

Back in 2004, when I worked as a teacher in London, I used to pick myself up a coffee and a muffin on my way into work every morning. It was my daily treat. I would then sit at my desk and catch up on emails and planning while having my on-the-go breakfast, before cracking on with prep and marking or whatever it was I needed to complete before my class was due to arrive. In those days I used to daydream about how wonderful it would be to actually pause and sit in the coffee shop where I bought my drink and muffin, having a leisurely breakfast before starting a day that was less hectic than mine usually were. The first morning I spent in a non-teaching job in London, I did exactly that. I arrived far too early for my new job and went and sat with my coffee and muffin for well over an hour, enjoying the shift in pace. It doesn't happen often, but I do try to remind myself every now and again, when everything feels a bit too hectic in my non-teaching world, that I do still have the headspace and physical time to sit with my coffee. That was my mindset shift, and I use it to remind myself why I moved away from the classroom and how, for me, it was a move for the better.

DOI: 10.4324/9781003378334-11

Transitioning through the trauma response

Surprisingly, you will find a move away from the classroom can feel quite traumatic:

- You will panic and feel real fear
- You will doubt yourself and experience imposter syndrome
- You will think many times about returning to the classroom (your safe space, especially if you have been teaching for many years)
- You will worry about money
- You will miss the children and the camaraderie of your fellow teachers

These things are all perfectly normal, but at the other end, there is a career that is just as fulfilling, but perhaps not quite as exhausting.

For this reason, I would genuinely encourage you to create your own transition process and make the shift a positive experience. Putting pen to paper can really help - consider the following questions to help you reflect on what you have been used to and how you will shift into a different routine and work headspace:

- What one thing would you like to add to your new routine that reminds you of the positive shift?
- What were your weekly hours at school?
- What will your new hours be, and how are they organised?
- How will you keep track of tasks to complete?
- What will your daily routines be going forward?
- How are you feeling? Track this!
- What do you love the most about teaching? How will you fill this gap?
- Who do you talk to or work closely with at work? How will you find this camaraderie in a new role or opportunity?
- Who can you tap into as a work buddy, if most of what you are going to do is quite isolated?
- Write down why you are opting for this change and why it is important - we quickly forget our past experiences and often look back with rose-tinted glasses.

Adjusting to a new working pattern

Teaching is an interesting profession in that, despite all the external asks, you essentially control your day. You plan it, and you run it. In other jobs it often isn't like this, which can be quite an adjustment.

New hours may well be flexible, especially if you are freelance, but will likely run later than you have been used to. Working from 8:00 to 4:30 or 9:00 to 5:30

is bog standard, which can feel strange if you have been used to an earlier start or a split in the afternoon. Usually the hours will be far more set than teaching, though, and there is unlikely to be an expectation for you to work outside of these hours. Oddly, this will need adjusting to as well – not working in the evenings or weekends will take quite a shift in your mindset. When I started work as an education officer at a local history museum, I remember very clearly being given a 50-page document with the instruction that I needed to read it, as it set out everything I needed to know about the department. I promptly popped it in my bag. My confused boss asked me why I had put it there. To read at home, obviously, I answered. She smiled and told me that I could sit and read it now, within my work hours. It took a while to get used to this, and sometimes I still catch myself saving things "to look at later", struggling to accept that I can do these things within work hours.

There may be more monotony in your role, or you may find yourself at the mercy of delegation and having to restructure your day at a moment's notice. But you will also find that your to-do list can usually wait until the morning, and that you are not commonly throwing 12-hour days just to tread water. You will also need to learn to manage a shifting workload that will require self-motivation. The upside is that you are already used to being flexible and changing things at a moment's notice, so this aspect of work away from a classroom will feel familiar.

You'll also need to pace yourself differently, as there will likely no longer be a six-week break in the summer or intermittent breaks throughout the year. Of course, for teachers these are not always breaks and, in fact, often make up for the ridiculous hours we tend to put in during term time. The joy derived from having five solid weeks of holiday (proper holiday, where you can switch off) and taking them whenever you please more than makes up for having less paid time off!

A change in colleagues

Think carefully about whom you spend most of your working life with when you are a teacher. It's the pupils. Yes, you have work colleagues who you interact with and collaborate with, but most of your day is filled with young people. Shifting from this to only interacting with adults, or with children with whom you don't have the opportunity to build a strong relationship, can be quite a challenge and often a shock. Just being aware of this will help. You will also have a different dynamic with colleagues and will need to work in teams and in isolation. Some will annoy you, and you can't get away from that, while others you will love but find you lose a lot of work time chatting with. You'll need to adjust to this new pattern.

A change in movement

Being a teacher is a lot more active than you might think (unless you work with very young children or teach PE, in which case, you will be fully aware of just how active you are on a daily basis). The shift from teaching to something that requires more desk work can find you sitting for prolonged lengths of time, with no trips to the staff room or another teaching space. You'll also find it is far easier to sit and snack without a class of children staring you down. Both of these things can have quite a profound impact on your health and need to be reflected on. Find a new routine that ensures you are still moving enough during the day and can stick to a healthy eating regime.

Boredom

One of the joys of teaching is that no two days are ever the same, and each day brings different challenges and learning opportunities. Non-teaching work can be really exciting and creative, but it can also be boring and repetitive, and some tasks or projects can be plain old dull. Sometimes this is actually quite nice, and I am the first person to put their hand up for an afternoon of "dull" when I am tired and my creative brain is exhausted, but when the dull is regular, you may need to remind yourself of why you moved on from your class-based job and to accept that, actually, sometimes boring is OK. Find ways to manage by mixing it up a bit, or, if you can, pop on a podcast or some music to help you push through.

Continuing to "make a difference"

Despite a change in direction and over a decade out of the classroom, I continue to have immense empathy and understanding for teachers. Working in education outside the classroom has certainly given me a more objective perspective on teaching, and yet I remain stalwart in my respect and admiration of those of you who remain in the classroom, working to improve the lives of thousands of children and offering wonderful learning opportunities and journeys for them. Teaching is a truly wonderful profession, and I am glad and proud to have been part of the teaching world, but I am also proud of the work I have done over the past decade, which has all been driven by a desire to support and help those colleagues working the long and gruelling hours of the teaching life.

When we leave the classroom, while there is often a sense of relief that your work-life balance has improved overnight, there is also a sense of loss that you are no longer "making that difference" that you feel when you are in a classroom. The teacher in you will always remain, and whatever you find yourself doing, you will always have that true understanding of grass-roots education and the impact it has. I have found that supporting teachers in whatever capacity you can enables you to continue to make a difference. I would highly recommend finding ways to keep hold of that and to feel you continue to have an impact on young people:

- Support local schools where you can, in whatever capacity
- Continue to be a sympathetic ear to teachers who remain in the profession
- Support organisations such as Education Support
- Become a school governor
- Keep up to date and informed with the realities of teaching by reading education publications such as TES, Schools Week, or the like

Teaching as a profession is like no other. You plan the lessons, you run the day, you have a constantly changing environment and list of tasks, and your job is very varied. Moving to other workspaces – both mentally and physically – can be challenging, but if you know what you are heading into and why you have chosen the change, it can also be very rewarding. In the final chapter we reflect back on our journey and look at the opportunities and paths that are right for you, recapping some of the key elements you need to consider for any kind of shift, be it large or small.

12   The dos and don'ts of work beyond the classroom

In this final chapter, we revisit the possible work forms we explored in Chapter One, highlighting the dos and don'ts of each one – a kind of quick-fix guide to side hustles, freelance roles, a business launch, and non-teaching employed roles. Whichever path you choose, make it an exciting one and cherry-pick the aspects of teaching you love and wish to keep, as well as the new skills and experiences you are keen to develop.

The side-hustler

Remember, a side hustle can be a great extra earner, but can also be the beginning of a new journey. You can build new skills, form a wider network, have a go at different professions, and test out your skills, all without compromising your current role. This is the safest way to test the waters.

Do

- Find something that excites you
- Look to do something you are good at or have an expertise in
- Use all of your own resources and nothing you use in school (physically and intellectually)
- Set aside time to complete this work in a way that doesn't make your day job more stressful
- Learn to say "no" or to push back deadlines or expectations if the task would take you well beyond your comfort zone
- Consider any ad hoc additional workloads from school (e.g. report writing or parent consultations)
- Price yourself well
- Talk to your headteacher about what you are doing

Don't

- Take on too much work all at once
- Use school resources or intellectual property
- Over-promise

DOI: 10.4324/9781003378334-12

- Offer to work for free or undervalue yourself
- Spend too much of your holiday time working on freelance projects

The part-time freelancer

Somewhere between a side-hustle and a freelance role, the part-time freelancer is a great way to experience the world of freelance without losing all of your employed security net. Whether you are looking for a change in pace for half of your week – one that offers full flexibility – or a gradual move into a full-time freelance role, this could be the perfect option for teachers taking a step outside of the classroom.

Do

- Find something that excites you
- Look to do something you are good at or have an expertise in
- Take care to ensure you are not creating a conflict of interest with your teaching work
- Check your contract to make sure you know what you can and cannot do
- Learn to say "no" or to push back deadlines or expectations if the task would take you well beyond your comfort zone
- Consider any ad hoc additional workloads from school (e.g. report writing or parent consultations)
- Price yourself well
- Set realistic deadlines
- Project-manage your work carefully
- Have an ongoing "pitching" process, or sign up/approach companies and organisations you'd like to work for
- Think carefully about your work set-up
- Ring-fence your freelance time to ensure school work doesn't take over
- Be nice to work with
- Meet your deadlines
- Produce work of a high standard
- Always offer to amend work if needed

Don't

- Take on too much work all at once
- Over-promise
- Use any school equipment or intellectual property in your work

- Complete freelance work when you are on a school work day
- Offer to work for free or undervalue yourself
- Take on projects that really don't appeal, unless money dictates otherwise
- Miss deadlines
- Send work that isn't checked
- Take offence if you are sent amends

The full-time freelancer

Are you ready to take the plunge into the world of fully flexible hours and total control over your work? While not for the faint-hearted, the fully freelance option is a liberating, fun ride that can ultimately lead to employed roles. You'll need to learn to network and sell yourself. You may also need to develop some new skills and qualifications, but the rewards can be high.

Do

- Find something that excites you
- Look to do something you are good at or have an expertise in
- Learn to say "no" or to push back deadlines or expectations if the task would take you well beyond your comfort zone
- Price yourself well
- Set realistic deadlines
- Project-manage your work carefully
- Have an ongoing "pitching" process, or sign up/approach companies and organisations you'd like to work for
- Try to find variety in the work you take on
- Think carefully about your work set-up
- Set clear work-home boundaries
- Take time to consider how you will manage financial changes and loss of perks
- Find a way to work that ensures you interact with others, avoiding isolation
- Be nice to work with
- Meet your deadlines
- Produce work of a high standard
- Always offer to amend if needed
- Ensure you continue to look for CPD opportunities

Don't

- Take on too much work all at once
- Over-promise

- Offer to work for free or undervalue yourself
- Take on projects that really don't appeal, unless money dictates otherwise
- Blur the boundaries between home time and work time
- Isolate yourself by only working from home
- Miss deadlines
- Send work that isn't checked
- Take offence if you are sent amends

The business launch

This is the ultimate option for those with a passion for something they want to own, but it requires a huge amount of effort, and there is nowhere to go when deadlines are looming or customer needs are urgent. Starting a business will demand a massive amount of mental and physical energy and may not initially earn you any money, and you will find yourself constantly "on". You may find yourself initially working more hours than you did in the classroom in order to make ends meet, but the rewards can be immense if you can make a success of your business.

Do

- Find something that excites you
- Look to do something you are good at or have an expertise in
- Look to find a business partner
- Take time to complete background research on your business venture
- Ensure you have the skills needed
- Come up with a business plan
- Price yourself well
- Ensure you still have an income stream external to your business

Don't

- Take on something for which there is too much competition (unless you have the edge)
- Have ambitions beyond your means in the early stages – these can come later
- Launch before you are fully ready
- Assume you'll make money or a salary in the first couple of years
- Become disheartened – learn to roll with the lows and celebrate the highs

The non-teaching employed role: full-time or part-time

If you need a guaranteed income and can't face the uncertainty that freelance work brings, finding a role that is in education but outside of the classroom could be the right option for you. You'll need to do your homework, though, and may need to build up some extra skills through a side hustle or training. But there are plenty of options out there. This is a great option if you want to go part-time in the classroom but need a salary for your non-teaching days.

Do

- Wait until the right job comes along
- Look to do something you are good at or have an expertise in
- Ensure your CV and covering letter are job-specific and don't present you as a packaged teacher
- Prepare yourself for a change in working dynamic and hours
- Have a career plan
- Reflect carefully on the day-to-day reality of specific roles
- Ask for a salary that reflects your worth (assuming your teaching expertise is key to the role)
- Try to take a week or two off between finishing teaching and starting a new role

Don't

- Take the first thing that comes along and see it as an escape – there always needs to be a pull on top of any potential push
- Shift into something that pays less if there is little promise of a potential pay increase
- Move into something that you know will bore you in a few years
- Take a new role without considering or finding out about the career prospects
- Assume your teaching experience ticks certain skills boxes without the need for explanation – make sure you apply for the job advertised
- Expect an equivalent pay offer to teaching – different sectors will have different pay scales, and while many jobs will try to entice teachers with an equivalent salary, you may need to build your experience in this new area before you reach that equivalence

How can I support you?

I hope this book has gone a long way in helping you reflect on your current role and the potential options available to you to work in the freelance education world or find an employed education role outside of the classroom. You can follow me on Twitter, Facebook, and Instagram for further support and ideas, or feel free to connect with me on LinkedIn. I run regular online sessions for teachers looking to take the leap and offer bespoke packages to support individuals. You can find me on the following:

- Instagram: @edu_beaver (Fe Luton Education)
- Twitter: @EduBeaver (Fe Luton Education)
- Facebook: Careers beyond the classroom (private group)
- LinkedIn: Fe Luton
- Website: www.careersbeyondtheclassroom.co.uk

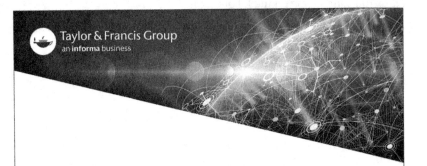

Printed in the United States
by Baker & Taylor Publisher Services